AF599232

StepParenting On Purpose

TRICIA SUESS CHARLESTON

Little Creek Press.
5341 Sunny Ridge Road
Mineral Point, WI 53565

ORDERING INFORMATION
Quantity sales. Special discounts are available on quantity purchases by corporations, associations, and others. For details, contact info@littlecreekpress.com

Orders by US trade bookstores and wholesalers.
Please contact Little Creek Press or Ingram for details.

Printed in the United States of America

Cataloging-in-Publication Data
Names: Suess Charleston, Tricia, author.
Title: 'Step'ping Up: StepParenting on Purpose / Tricia Suess Charleston
Description: Mineral Point, WI: Little Creek Press, 2024.
Identifiers: LCCN: 2024915640 | ISBN: 978-1-955656-81-8
Subjects: FAMILY & RELATIONSHIPS / Parenting / Stepparenting
FAMILY & RELATIONSHIPS / Alternative Family
FAMILY & RELATIONSHIPS / Chosen Family
SELF-HELP / Personal Growth / General

Book design by Little Creek Press

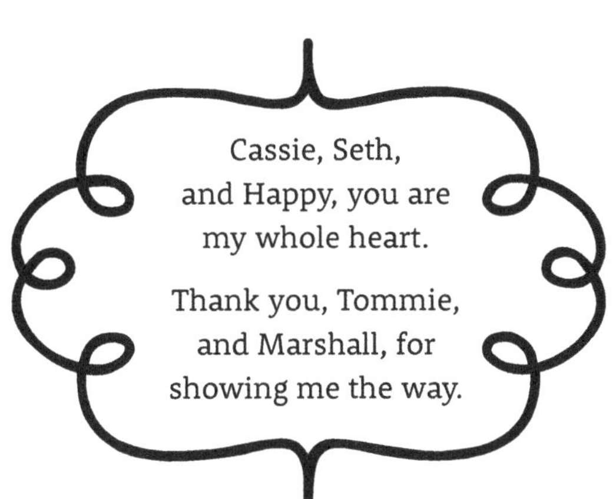

Cassie, Seth,
and Happy, you are
my whole heart.

Thank you, Tommie,
and Marshall, for
showing me the way.

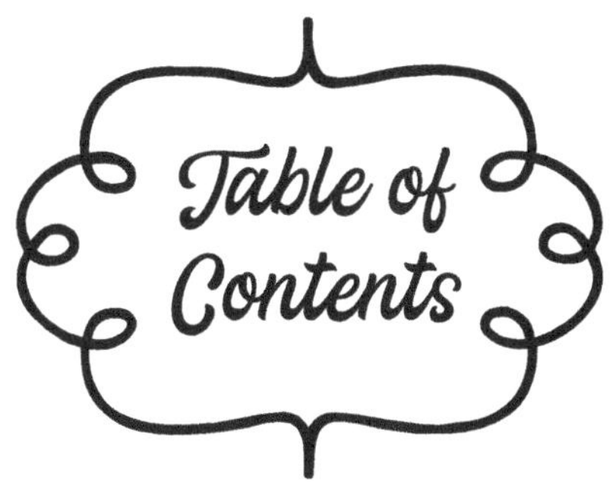
Table of
Contents

In Urban Dictionary, Slimshady420blazeit defines the verb “Stepping” like this:

To step means to go in general, but usually implies going to the next party.

M: shit, is everyone stepping?

D: yeah man let’s step

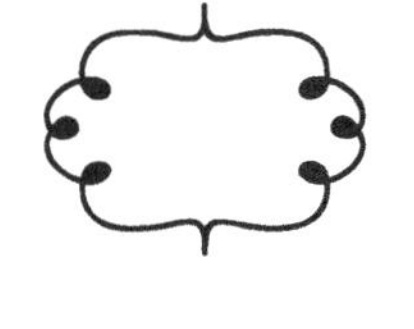

Introduction

"So, do you have any brothers or sisters?"

I sigh a little inside whenever someone asks me this question. Sometimes I chuckle and counter with, "How much time do you have?" I don't mean to be flip. It's just that I have a long and convoluted answer to this innocent small-talk question.

"Well, I have two sisters, a half-brother, a half-sister, and five stepbrothers." My listener's eyes usually get really big at this point. I always wonder to myself why I feel the need to differentiate my half-siblings. I don't like that I do that. I'm a literal and detailed person, though, and I want to be accurate in my labeling. And, if I'm honest with myself, I get more of a reaction listing my sibs that way. Throwing the "halfs" in there makes it more dramatic.

As impressive as the answer is, it leaves out the three stepsisters and one stepbrother I had from my second StepMom.

Okay, wait. What now? I told you. It's convoluted.

I have a LOT of experience with Step relationships. Some of those relationships have been highly challenging. Some have created a joy in my life that I thought I could never have. I'm grateful for them all. They taught me how to be an awesome StepMother.

And I love being a StepMother.

That's right. I said it.

I know I'm not supposed to love being a Step—Cinderella and all that.

But I love being a StepMom. It has turned out to be one of the greatest happinesses of my life, and I'm good at it. I can feel that I am. I see it in how my StepKids interact with me, and I know it because they tell me.

Now, getting to that level took a minute because we all had to figure each other out. In this context, a "minute" equals two or three or five years. And our relationships continue to develop.

StepParenting was weird and scary at first. I didn't have kids of my own, but we were still blending families—my family of one with my husband's family of four. Plus Ted the dog. I wanted so desperately to do this job well. Some of the things I did were spot on. Some of them, not so much. But it all came from my experiences as a StepDaughter.

If you want to do this job well, too, you'll gain tips and strategies from this book to help you navigate the relationship. Success is built from past challenges as long as you're willing to learn from them.

I've worked really hard to get to this fulfilling place where I'm a part of a family that loves and stands by each other, and I want to be an example for you and your family.

You'll read about things you should say to your StepKids and things that should never be said. You'll learn the dos and don'ts of StepParenting. (Two big dos: Get yourself right before marriage and watch your words.) You'll learn how I built this life and see how it worked for me and how it can work for you.

Part I covers your relationship with yourself. You'll read about making yourself whole so that you can give your best to your marriage and your new family.

Part II will discuss the relationships you develop with your StepKids. Just as with parents, your relationships will be different with each kid.

Part III explores developing all of you into a family unit. What does that look like, and how do you get there?

I'm inspired daily by my Step life and the love I've found in these extra-familial relationships. You'll find in these pages the joy and heartache and love I've discovered being in this role.

You'll hear about how much of a blessing my family is to me and the joys I've embraced being a part of it. It is truly incredible to influence the life of a kid—there's a lot of power there. You'll learn to show up, ask for what you need, and be an adult in your household.

Hopefully, you'll find yourself in these words and that what you read here will make your life as a StepParent easier and more rewarding, because your StepKids deserve it.

This book is about the relationships between StepParents and StepChildren. There won't be any discussion about blending kids together. It's coming from the point of view of a StepDaughter who grew into a StepMother. Most of what you'll read will relate to StepFathers, StepMothers, or StepParents in general.

My StepMothering perspective comes from having StepKids who were teenagers and young adults when we met. While I was never a StepMom to little kiddos, I was definitely a kiddo with StepParents (starting at age eight). All of those StepKid experiences have made me the StepMom I am today.

I did not include any child development science or psychology of relationships. There aren't any studies, clinicians, or child development research aside from the studies and research I did on my own life.

Rather, this book describes my approach to StepParenting based on my vast experience as a StepKid.

I've had several StepMoms and one StepDad, and frankly, they weren't all joyful experiences. What kid loves everything their parents do? Sometimes, they showed me things I didn't want to do. They mostly showed me the right way to walk into this role.

This book is about my approach and how you can consciously craft your own techniques to help create a happy, healthy family. My approach has been based on my experience as a StepKid, a significant amount of introspection, on my StepParent examples, on a desire to do this job well, and the wisdom to marry a good man who loves being a parent.

I took all of my challenging StepKid experiences, combined them with my awesome StepKid experiences, wrapped them up into my own StepParenting style, and created for myself a nifty little StepFamily that I'm thankful for every single day.

You may have noticed the capitalization and lack of space in the Step titles. That's on purpose. These relationships deserve to be capitalized. They're special and sometimes crazy or hard, but they'll all touch your heart. StepParents play a huge role in kids' lives, and regular old "stepmother" doesn't do that justice. We're StepMoms! We're in it. We're capitalizing that shit.

I have been looking for ways to shorten these words, and I asked my StepKids if I could combine "Step" and "Kids" into "SKids." I thought it was hilarious—they didn't necessarily agree. I still do it privately, though, so you will see SKids in the book. Maybe it'll catch on.

Cropping "StepMom" comes out "SMom," which isn't so bad. It gets a little more tricky if you're writing "StepMother" that way because then it just comes out "SMother." So we're still working on that one. But we need updated and cool ways to convey these relationships and bring these titles into the present day, where Stepping is increasingly common.

MY STEP HISTORY

I have forty-three years of experience in Step relationships. My parents divorced when I was seven, and my dad married my first StepMother when I was eight, back in 1979. That relationship started out fun (she made fondue!) but was difficult for most of our time together. She and my dad had two kids. It was fun having babies around, and I enjoyed helping care for them and watching them grow.

After my StepMom passed in 1996, my dad married my second StepMother. Those two didn't have any kids together, and that marriage dissolved after a few years. Now he's married to my third (and final!) wonderful StepMother, Tommie. They've been married since 2010, and she's been a grand addition to our family.

My mom married my StepFather, Marshall, in 1985, which feels like a lifetime ago. They're still married more than thirty years later. Marshall has been a stalwart presence since day one. He's a caring man who works hard and wants the best for his family.

My StepMom, Tommie, and StepDad, Marshall, have been my primary guides as I have taken my own StepMother journey. Through their caring examples, they've shown me the path I wanted to take.

I met my husband, Jason, in 2016, and we married in 2018, so I've been a StepMother to Cassie, Seth, and Happy since then. They're all adults now but were teens and young adults when we met. They were just starting to launch their own lives.

Talk about a tough time to enter a family. Teenagers aren't known for their kind, considerate natures. But this was perfect for me. I always secretly wished I could "get a kid" about twelve years old when they're fully caring for their own bodies (meaning, no poop to deal with) and can have great conversations with me.

We worked through those teen years together and now enjoy each other as adults. It's been quite a journey, and I look forward to every next step.

I include my StepParents when I say "my parents." They *are* my parents. They guide me and support me and love me just like my mom and dad do. I have four parents, no question. And I hope my StepKids feel the freedom to think of me that way, too. StepParents aren't replacement parents. They're additional parents.

Not everyone wants additional parents. Not all parents are awesome, and not all StepParents care. But lots of us do.

PART ONE
You

The StepParent Stigma

"What comes to mind when you think of the word *Mother*?"

In a presentation about StepParenting, I asked the audience this question. The answers were as expected: educator, nurturer, caregiver, loving, comforter, friend, and your biggest fan.

These wonderful descriptions evoke a sense of love and feel comforting and supportive, like a perfect cup of cocoa to warm your hands as you snuggle into a blanket on a cold winter night.

The next question: "What words come to mind when you think of the word *StepMother*?" Again, the answers were as expected: scary, evil, new rules.

The group had trouble coming up with more. When prompted, and because they knew the topic of the presentation, they finally came up with *supporter* and *guidance*. Those sounded much better but weren't the group's automatic responses. Those words didn't flow like *nurturer* for mother or *evil* for StepMother.

That's what we're dealing with here. There's a stigma about StepParents brought on by the fairy tales we were told over and over as kids and perpetuated in our culture. It shows up in movies, on television—I'm looking at you, Lifetime channel—and in nicknames like "step-monster."

After hearing the stories of Cinderella, Snow White, Hansel and Gretel, and others, it's no surprise that *evil*, *scary*, and *new rules* were the first words that came to mind when thinking of StepMothers. This perception has been instilled in our culture.

(Can you think of a fairy tale where the StepMother says, "Dear StepDaughter, I love you so much. You are a valued and important member of this family. Here, have the best food and the finest dresses. I'm definitely not sending a huntsman after you into the woods to bring me back your heart.")

The entry for StepMother in *Wikipedia* affirms this cultural issue. StepParents also face societal challenges due to the stigma around the evil StepMother character, and that did not escape me. That narrative was a big part of our most beloved stories growing up. Follow that up with my challenging relationship with my first StepMother, and now the concept—that stigma—is fully installed.

Going through adulthood, I began facing situations where I could potentially be a StepMother myself, and I. Was. Terrified. It's not that kids are so bad. They take a little getting used to if you're not around them regularly, but all the kids I encountered were pretty cool. It was all me. I was so scared of repeating the cycle, perpetuating the stereotype, and creating a difficult relationship with a kid.

I discussed my fears with these kids' fathers along the way, and they all assured me that I couldn't possibly be mean to a kid. I loved that they were so sure, because I wasn't. I had never been in that situation, and I didn't know how I would react. Would I fixate on the man and resent the kids for being a part of our relationship? Would I have little patience and understanding of what their lives might be like? Would I let my own troubles and fears spill out onto them?

Ultimately, I chose to go forward. I met a man who was worth the journey and helped me every step of the way through the transition into StepParenting. As we traveled down this road together, our relationship deepened. I got to know the kids more, and we began to figure out how we were going to be in a family together. After some time, I asked Jason, out of the blue, "Can I just freely love my StepKids?"

"Yes, I hope that you do."

Weird but okay. Let's give that a try.

Sometimes I wish we had a different word for StepMother. There's so much weight and connotation behind that word that belies the joyful experience I've found it to be. I've heard from countless others about their own quality, life-affirming Step relationships. My experience isn't unique, but it also isn't openly discussed in our society. You might raise an eyebrow when you hear a StepParent or a StepKid speak very lovingly about their Step. It's not the norm we're presented with.

And when you hear a kid mention a StepParent, there's a little twitch of concern in the back of your mind, wondering if and hoping that the Step is treating them well. We generally don't have that concern with "regular" parents.

Based on the messages we receive and my own experience, it felt like Step relationships shouldn't end up really happy. It's *supposed* to be challenging, right? Or maybe you're okay with each other, but it's perhaps not necessarily a loving relationship.

I had to change my beliefs about what a StepMother could be. I had to change my beliefs about how I could show up in that role. And I had to change my identity from someone who was scared of this relationship to someone who could have confidence and learn and grow within it. I had to decide for myself, outside of cultural ideas and outside of my own history, how I wanted to feel and how I wanted to show up in my own family.

When you love being a Step, when you love your SKids, you're going counterculture. You have to work through the stigma and find your truth. Forget about what our culture dictates "should" be. You get to decide what relationships you want with your SKids and how you talk about those relationships with others.

You can be a part of the movement that changes our society's perceptions of what it means to be in Step relationships. When people hear more loving stories about Steps, enough to drown out the whole Cinderella bit, you'll start seeing a shift in perception. At that point, it should be a lot easier to shout out loud how much you love your SKids. Until then, you may have to do it without societal support.

Even as I've loved my own SKids deeply, it took me a long time to make any declaration that I loved being a Step. That's just not what society tells us to do. If I'm being honest, it still feels weird that I'm in this cohesive, loving family unit that I entered into later in life. I'm still working through eschewing culture and forgetting what's "supposed" to happen so I can freely love my family without reservation. But the work is well worth it.

I love being a StepMom. I'll speak highly of my SKids as long as anyone will listen. And then I'll keep the conversation going with myself when everyone else stops listening. These kids are cool. Our relationships are cool. Stepping is cool, people.

Your Relationship with Yourself

I know. I've only been married for four years, so how qualified am I to give marriage advice? Plenty qualified, actually. Taking only my current marriage into account disregards twenty-nine years of figuring out how it *doesn't* work. And I studied it very closely.

I dated here and there. There weren't many serious relationships in all those years outside a two-year marriage in the nineties (which doesn't even count anymore) and a three-year relationship in my early forties. But in each encounter, I learned something about myself and what I was willing to allow in my life. There was so much process of elimination that it seemed there was hardly anything left to make a partner out of. But in walked Jason Charleston, saying all the right things. It was as if I had built him in a lab.

How could this man be so right for me after a couple of decades of giving my time to men who weren't? My relationships before him were not the fairy-tale, life-giving type from the Hallmark movies, that's for sure. (I don't mean to disparage others. If you've been down the dating road, you know what I mean.)

To what do I attribute this dramatic turn-around in the quality of romantic prospects? I got square with myself. I got to a place where

I was full and happy and really enjoying myself. I loved being single and had a whole plan built around it. I made my life into one that I enjoyed. All those other men before that point were on par with where I was in my life and my head at those times—not quite ready to be loved fully.

MAKING YOURSELF RIGHT BEFORE MARRIAGE

Living that experience led me to the best relationship advice I have to offer: make yourself right first. I don't mean to make yourself perfect, but I do mean to put yourself first. Get your shit together so you can give quality life energy to your partner and your family. You've probably read the quotes: "Fill your own cup first" and "Put on your own oxygen mask first." You have to dedicate time to making yourself into the person you always knew you could be. Then that awesomeness can spill out on everyone around you instead of unacknowledged pain.

It's a win-win because the more square you are with yourself, the more fully you know and accept yourself, the less bullshit you'll be willing to put up with in a relationship and in another person.

When you're in the market for a life partner, self-care works at the macro level by putting yourself in a place to attract the person your heart is calling for. It works at the micro level when you're in that relationship, and it's time to maintain and grow that bond between you and your partner.

Does it sound like a big task? It should, because it is. Focusing on yourself and learning to accept all the different parts of you should be considered a part of your overall health plan. Going to the gym a few times a week, eating vegetables every day, practicing good hygiene, and spending some time reading, journaling, or meditating will all support your continued growth.

Consider it a maintenance item. You go to the gym to keep your muscles and heart strong. You spend time on yourself to keep your spirit strong.

I have a problem with being overly critical of myself and everyone around me. I like to think I keep it under wraps pretty well, but I don't know that those closest to me would agree. At the same time, I've worked hard to find peace within myself and give myself and others the grace to be human. But I can tell when I'm out of whack by my thoughts about Jason. When I feel short and annoyed with him, I know I'm unhappy with something in myself. He's not doing anything differently; he's a very consistent person. So when I find fault in what he's doing, it's actually about me. I'm finding fault in me, and it's bubbling up as fault in the person I care most about in the whole world.

I'm thankful for this subtle cue that shows up as automatic thoughts. "Jeez, why is Jason doing that thing like that?" Or, "Why is he asking me about this?" These small thoughts sour my outlook. I try not to say them out loud, though I haven't been perfect.

But when I listen to those thoughts—when I finally pick up on the cue—it serves as a great reminder to (a) chill out, (b) get my priorities straight, (c) get back to a place of thankfulness, and (d) figure out where my cognitive dissonance is that's causing all the internal criticism.

I've apologized to Jason several times throughout our relationship for being critical. He says he doesn't notice, but I think he's just being kind. Or maybe I'm doing okay at keeping my mouth shut when I have those thoughts. It's probably that he's being kind.

Either way, critical thoughts don't serve me. Even if I did express them, I'm not doing Jason any favors. It's not like he'll suddenly do everything exactly how I would from now on because I made a snippy comment. That's not how things work. Nobody likes to be criticized. It's not all that great for the criticizer, either. I'm angry, sad, annoyed, and bitter in that mode. Who wants that?

So when I ask myself why on earth he would be doing that thing, that's my cue to go inside myself and straighten myself out. After all, Jason got along just fine for forty-three years before we met. He doesn't need me to tell him what to do. (Every time I read this sentence, I cringe at how much I *do* tell him what to do. It's a work in progress.)

My biggest trick for turning my attitude around is to pause and breathe. This is a great strategy for almost any situation. The first step in the pause is to reframe the critical attitude I have toward Jason. He doesn't deserve that. I remind myself to return to a place of gratitude for this amazing man who just wants to love me.

The second step is to figure out why I feel critical. What am I doing, thinking, or feeling that's causing me to feel critical of myself? What judgment am I applying? What do I think I'm doing wrong?

Sometimes the answer is that I feel guilty because I think I'm not doing enough or too much of something. Or I'm not feeling the "correct" way about a situation. Whatever it is, criticism will not be effective in helping turn it around. A bold accounting of the thing that's bothering me is the answer.

Do I have a bad attitude because I've simply decided to? That's an easy fix— make a different decision (gratitude is helpful for this one). Am I feeling unsure of myself at work? Could there be a big presentation or speech that I'm subconsciously nervous about? Or do I need a nap or some food (also an easy fix)?

None of that stuff has anything to do with Jason. Criticism outward is criticism inward.

You may notice that the answer is never more criticism. I can't shame myself into changing. So I either apply grace when I am doing fine and need to lay off myself and grab some peace. Or, I look for ways to adjust whatever I'm doing that's eliciting judgment. Either way, the criticism stops once the solution has been presented.

You know the saying about how we're our own worst critic? No doubt! But we're just regular people, and while we can expect greatness from ourselves, we will never be perfect. It's about progress, not perfection, and that's where grace comes in.

When I'm not square with myself, I can't be square with Jason or anyone else.

I'm not trying to be perfect over here, but I am trying to give my best to the person I am building a life with. I am working to ensure that my partner gets the best I have to offer. I miss sometimes, but as long as I keep myself pointed forward and clear the garbage in my brain, I'm doing just fine. And it shows in our relationship.

How does self-care affect SKids?

You know how sometimes you're worried about something at work, or you have a cold, or you're just plain tired, and then the people in your house need to eat and want your attention, and if you have little kiddos, they require even more. Maybe you snap a little or even yell because you JuSt CaN't TaKe It AnYmOrE. When you live your day-to-day in a status quo—getting up, doing the work, going to bed, doing it again the next day—it's easy to let these external circumstances take over your patience and peace.

But when you give yourself the tools to remind yourself of who you are, to pause and breathe, to practice putting things in perspective, you can bring yourself back to gratitude, to finding the joy in your home.

Grace and peace don't just magically show up in your life. You must actively cultivate them. And when you don't foster grace and peace, the opposite will take up residence. Something is going to be there—either the thing you chose intentionally or the thing you didn't.

Grace and peace can be cultivated by reading (or listening to) self-development books, having coaches or mentors, meditating, journaling—anything that means you're prioritizing your own peaceful mind. When you are well, everyone around you benefits.

Your internal state will spill out onto the people around you no matter what. People in your life will feel it when you're cranky, tired, and low on patience. Similarly, those in your life will feel it when you're thankful, peaceful, and happy. Which would you rather deliver? Only you can take responsibility for your physical, mental, and spiritual health by taking real-world action. Magic happens in your life when you know yourself and step into that knowing.

When I'm square with myself, I can show my SKids what a strong, independent, self-possessed woman looks like. I can be an example for them of a healthy person in a healthy relationship. I can bring my best self into their lives. I offer better advice, I have broader perspectives, I have more patience, and I experience a more profound gratitude.

I recently experienced a time of frustration and anger. I was fed up with a circumstance I'd accepted as fact for my whole life. Despite my best efforts, I spent nearly a month feeling ineffective in this emotional, sad place. The emotions were there, and as I worked on figuring that out so I could move on from it, I also had to work on maintaining my relationships despite my feelings.

That sorrowful sense had nothing to do with my family. Jason supported me and trusted me to find my way through it. And once I did, I emerged stronger and more resolute than ever.

All the while, I did not do a perfect job of spilling only positives on the people around me. I was mopey. I was not as zesty as usual. My energy was taken up with figuring out what was happening and moving through it. I used my tools—journaling, self-coaching, talking with trusted confidants—and even then, it took time to work it all out.

That won't be the last time it happens, either. Trials are a part of life. Here are a few tips to begin finding grace and peace:

- Start working with a life coach and then actually follow their advice.
- Read self-development books (or listen to audiobooks). Ten pages a day, which takes about ten minutes, will get you through a book per month. If you don't think you have time, try listening to an audiobook during your commute to and from work or when working around the house. (Check the appendix for a list of my favorite books.)
- Start really hearing the thoughts in your head. Do they support you? Do they bring peace? If not, change them up. You get to pick what you think.

PRO TIP: There are no thought police. When you ease up and start feeling better about yourself, no one can say, "Hey now, you're supposed to feel bad about yourself; you better cut that happy business out." I'll say it again—your thoughts are completely your choice. Choose thoughts that support you and move you forward.

- Eat a vegetable. They're pretty good, and your body loves them.
- Sleep, my friend. There is no nobility in depriving your body of its most precious rest.
- Get some nature. Watch a campfire, really feel the wind on your face, put your feet in some water, touch a tree, or have a plant in your house. Nature is healing and rejuvenating. While you're there, fully embrace it. Get all woo and try to be one with it, whatever that means for you.

BALANCING MARRIAGE AND FAMILY

When you get yourself right, when you know who you are, and when your bullshit tolerance is low (that means you don't put up with it in your own brain and you're selective about who and what you let into your life), then you can go heart-first into your new family.

You're not marrying an individual; you're marrying a family. And that family needs each other. Eventually, they'll need you, too, but that will take time. The kids' activities and their needs all come first. It isn't about you; it's about kids who need their parents. Had you been with them all along, this would be a natural and normal part of your life. But when you come in later, you have to flex and recognize that they had their own lives with their parents before you came along, and they still need things that children need.

This will be a much easier flow if you feel strong within yourself. If you don't feel strong, it can be easy to let family life spark jealousy. This is not to say that your spousal relationship gets no attention. That's not healthy for anyone. You're aiming for balance. Yes, it's okay to have a date night. Sometimes your date night will be a youth baseball game in another town. Embrace it.

You are marrying a family who will be your family at least as long as you are married, and sometimes even longer, depending on the relationships you build. You'll be celebrating birthdays, anniversaries, weddings, babies, and all the fun stuff. You'll be helping and listening and supporting when things are tough for the kids.

And you'll be helping and listening and supporting your spouse when they're worried about their kids. My StepMom says, "You're only as happy as your saddest child," which I've found to be true. Your spouse is going to be worried about their kids, and that means some of their brain space is dedicated to people and situations that are not you. This is good—you shouldn't be their whole life anyway.

The kids are not going away. They will be a permanent part of your life. If you think, *Oh yeah, the kids are great and all, but they'll move out someday, and then we'll have our lives to ourselves.* That's not how it works. You'll always have an uphill battle if you don't embrace the whole family.

It's the long haul, and honestly, It's pretty cool. Whole families are like a built-in team. Lean into that team, and lend your wholeness to it. It's no fun when someone is clearly part of a group but doesn't participate. Be a full participant in your family.

HEALING YOUR PAST

People come into our lives for a variety of reasons, whether it's to teach us things for the purpose of growth or to help us heal past hurts. I've found this to be true with many folks who have come into my life. Some fulfilled their purpose, and then we moved down different paths. Some of them have stayed, and they keep showing me how I can be better, and I'm so thankful for those people.

I had a beautiful opportunity to help heal past hurts when Cassie entered my life.

Cassie has always reminded me of myself in my early twenties. I look back on that time in my life with fondness and a bit of sadness. I had a great time and was also all over the place, with no real direction. I didn't put much effort into college, so I stopped going and worked a bunch of different jobs, but I always paid my bills and always looked forward.

Enter this young woman now showing me bits of myself from that time. Vibrant, unsure, trying really hard, kind of scared, and working to figure everything out.

Here's my chance! I can make Cassie into the me I never was at that age. I'm going to say exactly the right thing to her, and then she will become the me that I never was and show me how it could have been. Ah, the glory, the joy, the sureness that this will generate! I can now fill the gaps in my heart by making this young woman's life exactly what I think it should be.

I thought I was going to fix twenty-one-year-old Tricia by "fixing" my twenty-one-year-old StepDaughter. No.

Cassie isn't me. She's her own person with her own beliefs, experiences, and thoughts. I love how she shows me parts of myself; these are merely reflections, though, and not an assignment of my life onto hers. And there are no magic words that will turn her into me. Thank goodness for that because she has her own light to shine.

Trying to apply the perspective of a fifty-year-old onto someone with less than half the amount of life experience is also an exercise in futility. It's unrelatable. It doesn't translate.

My attempts at trying to heal my past by making her life (my version of) perfect resulted in frustration that my words didn't magically transform her life. It's like at graduation ceremonies, where there are many speakers and, as a seasoned adult, you can appreciate what they're saying. I even gave Maria Shriver a solo standing ovation when I saw her speak at the University of Michigan's graduation ceremony. But the students just hear noise. They can't relate. They're thinking about other things and just want the ceremony to be over so they can finally get their diplomas.

It's like that. I can lay down all the wisdom I can muster, but I'm still a kind-of parent, so my advice is received as such, and kids still have to go through some shit to figure that stuff out.

We will all be confronted with old wounds—that's life as a human—and we have the opportunity to heal them, but we must use caution.

These kids aren't Past Me. I can't heal myself by changing them. But I have the most wonderful opportunity to offer them those things I wish I'd had—an encouraging word, a peaceful household, a home where their friends are welcome.

Think about something you wish your parents would have provided for you and do that for someone else.

REFLECTION QUESTIONS

- What is one thing I can do to bring myself more peace?
- What can I learn from my new family to help me heal my past hurts?
- How can I support my SKids and give them those things I wish I'd had?
- What tools can I implement to turn my attitude around, no matter how small?

PART TWO:
Them

Your Relationship with Your SKids

The StepParent-StepChild relationship is created together, and it can't be rushed or forced. I learned this from my StepParents, who showed me the way, sometimes by showing me what I did not want to do. I owe them all a debt of gratitude for paving the way for me to step into this role. I'm so thankful to have their examples to guide me.

StepParents may be becoming more common, but I suspect few have had the benefit of having their own StepParents to show them what this is all about. We all have parents and use examples from our upbringing when raising our children. Sometimes we discover ourselves doing the same things without even realizing it. You say a phrase, then stop short: *When did my mom get here? Whoa.*

My StepMom, Tommie, and StepDad, Marshall, really laid the groundwork for me. I didn't have to invent anything. I just followed their examples.

Tommie's approach may not have been purposeful, but mine is, and it's primarily based on Tommie's model. Well, except that Tommie cooks a lot, and it took me about a year to cook anything beyond tater tots. Everything else was there, though.

I take it step by step, little by little. I go to the events, arrange the get-togethers, and participate in the family. I cheer my SKids on, listen to their stories, and encourage their time with their dad. I hang back and let them build their relationship with me rather than try to bring it about before its time. I'm just there for them, and I always try to be myself.

Hanging back was really hard when I desperately wanted my SKids' approval. But it was necessary. I was entering an established family. They'd had years together to figure each other out. I couldn't just pop in and take over. I had to get the lay of the land first. Let them show me how things work in their family.

I believe that Marshall was just being Marshall—kind, integrous, steady. He worked a lot (still does), but he was also always there. I wouldn't have described us as close, but I knew he cared. Marshall always believed in me, which I'm unfortunately only recently figuring out.

What is StepParenting like? What even is this relationship? StepParenting is all the best stuff about parenting. That's it. It's like being a parent, but I don't have to discipline (depending on the Parenting Agreement—more on that later). I get to love and support without needing to direct and correct. I'm a guide and a resource, and I'm family. My husband, my StepKids, and I are a team. We cheer each other on and wish the best for each other.

I also feel the heartache that "real" parents feel when I hope every day that I'm doing the right thing. I give the same sigh of relief that real parents give when I know the kids are home safe for the night. I feel the frustrations of real parents when the kids are not doing what I think they should be. I feel the pride that real parents feel when I see my kids on stage, at the plate, or working hard at whatever they're doing. I feel the sting that real parents feel when I think about the youngest moving out on his own.

I missed the years when these kids were little. I never changed their diapers. I didn't see their first steps or hear their first words. I didn't take their pictures on the front step every first day of school. Every once in a while, my experience with these kids makes me wonder if I really missed something special by not having kids of my own. But these kids *are* my kids. They're the kids of my heart. I'm not a bio-mom or even an adopted mom. But I am an "other mom." I'm a StepMom. I love them deeply. They are part of who I am.

Indeed, these kids have made me a better person. When kids enter your life, all of a sudden, there are these eyes watching everything you do, taking their examples from you. That'll make you straighten right up. It sure had that effect on me. The Charlestons gave me a space and a reason to do better and to be better.

My StepKids like and respect me, and I them. They're good people who work hard and look forward. They're fun and funny, and they get after life.

I have different relationships with each of them, and we enjoy each other differently. These Charlestons show up for each other. They help each other. They love each other. It's been so long since I've been in a family unit like that that I'd forgotten what it was like. It's pretty great.

It's easy to say all these things a few years in with some time and practice under my belt. It took time for our relationships to develop, as all relationships do. And there were a couple of bumps at first, but we figured it out together.

So, yes. They're MY kids. I didn't birth them, I didn't raise them, but they're still my kids. They're the kids in my life, and I love them so much it hurts.

We raised a glass over Christmas Eve brunch, and I had this whole bit planned out. My toast would be: "You may not be the children of my loins, but you are the children of my heart." And they would groan and say, "Oh, Tricia," as they rolled their eyes because I had referenced my loins, and no kid wants to think about any parent's loins. It would be funny.

My toast began. Get ready for some yuks. "You may not be the children of my loins, but you are the children of my heart." They all responded with a very sweet and loving "Aww." No groaning, no eye rolls, just a whole bunch of love and the *thud* of plastic cups coming together in cheers. Those kids.

I used to wish we had a different term for StepMom that conveyed the relationships I have with my StepKids and that many StepParents have as well. We love our StepKids. The connotations from the fairy tales and the very real-life tales of stepmothers who aren't so great can cloud the StepMom title. But I don't wish for that anymore. I love being a StepMom, and I'm proud of it. I'm owning the word.

Step relationships are cool because their prevalence is fairly new, so we still get to make up our own definitions.

There are fairly defined expectations of parents, grandparents, and siblings. Inside these relationships, you pretty well know what you'll get. In general, we have shared experiences with parents, grandparents, and siblings.

But StepParenting is still new enough that those expectations are unformed, or stories have influenced our current views of StepParents, as we saw earlier. Because of this, we get to define these relationships for ourselves and with each Step singularly.

While talking with my own StepMom, Tommie, about being in this role, she said that sometimes she wants to reach out and hug her StepKids and tell them everything is going to be fine. But she holds back because she wants to be careful about not appearing as though she's vying for the mom position—trying to be our mom. I can relate to this feeling and have struggled with it myself, especially in the beginning.

But over time, we've all figured out that there's room for everyone. It's okay for my SKids to love their mom and me at the same time. It's okay for me to look to Tommie for guidance as I do with my mom. StepParents become this gift of another parent-like resource. It's all the best stuff about parenting.

Even though they're not my biological kids, and I can never know what it's like to love someone in that way, I experience moments of it.

I feel it when someone has wronged one of them, and I want to rise up and strike that person down with a fiery spear through their rotten hearts for hurting my family. I feel it when the Charlestons circle the wagons against that enemy, and I'm there, arm-in-arm with them. I feel it when we're all together, and they start joking with each other, and our family unit grows even closer. I feel it when they ask me for advice or just want to talk through something.

Loving these children brings an ache in my heart I've never known before and an equally intense love. These may not be my children, but they're my people. They're my family.

For years before the Charlestons, I had fancied skipping all that diaper-changing business and "getting a kid at age twelve." And wouldn't you know it, that's what happened. I bypassed all the baby and young kid phases and came onto the scene when they were nearly adults.

But I didn't exactly "get a kid." The Step relationship is different. It's not automatic; it has to be nurtured and earned. Okay, technically, it's automatic in title, but if you want the kind of relationship that makes your heart ache, you have to work for that.

Quoting the book *The Power of Moments* by Chip Heath and Dan Heath: "Relationships don't deepen naturally. In the absence of action, they will stall." It takes focused action to create deep relationships. Sometimes it's hard, but hard things are usually worth it, and relationships that feed your soul are absolutely worth it.

Step relationships are their own thing. We're not really a parent, but we kind of are. We're not the cool aunt, but we kind of are. That's part of what makes it so wonderful. It's its own thing. With each StepKid, we define for ourselves what that relationship will be. I suppose a savvy parent works in the same way, tailoring each relationship to the needs and personalities of each kid.

As I proceeded through my twenties and thirties (and into my forties), there were always a few "parent things" I wished I could experience with my own children. I was okay with not having these, but I also knew I would treasure them if given the chance.

One of these "parent things" was being an involved parent of a high schooler. As a kid, I saw these parents and, at times, through adulthood, and I had always wondered what it would be like to bake cookies for the bake sale, sell tickets at the basketball game, and know all your teenager's friends and their parents.

My wish came true the summer before Seth entered his junior year.

SETH

About four months into my relationship with Jason, Seth auditioned for and was accepted into a folk-dancing group in high school made up of mainly juniors and seniors who learn a catalog of old-timey Scandinavian folk dances and then tour around performing shows in full bunad costumes. (Bunads are traditional Norwegian clothes.) They perform about sixty times during the school year, begin rehearsals before school starts in the fall, and rehearse every morning before school. It's pretty intense for the students and parents alike.

I had a loose understanding of how involved the dancer's parents were expected to be, and I knew Jason's work would limit his availability.

(The amount of time, energy, and effort parents put into their kids' activities was a big adjustment for me. My last experience with this was when I was a kid performing in concerts and plays. I know my parents came to the shows, but I don't remember them being required to volunteer like parents are today. The stories our memories tell us are unreliable, so I could have a very skewed idea of how it was in the eighties. Still, I was quite surprised and taken aback at how much time and energy kids' activities require from both kids and their parents. But I digress.)

Holy smokes, cue the whirlwind! Meetings (bring your checkbook, folks), sign-ups, performances, dinners, festivals, parades, and more! The Stoughton Norwegian Dancers is an intense group requiring significant investments of time and money from the families whose kids were lucky enough to make it.

I remember sitting in my work office and getting the news from a community member that my new boyfriend's son had made it into the group. "Let me know if you need any help baking." Uhhh ... baking? What?

Well, yes, thank you. I DO need help baking—A LOT of help, actually. People in the community, my sister, and even the Pick 'n Save grocery store came through for me with all the baking.

Dancer parents have lots of jobs. We made lefse, baked cookies, drove the kids to their performances, decorated semitrailers for parades, planned social gatherings, packed snacks, wrote checks, made and served meatballs, made lapskaus (beef stew), and there must be at least three more things I'm forgetting.

This group was a well-oiled machine. The jobs were concise and clear, with well-established processes. Just learn from the senior parent who did it last year, and you'll be fine. It bears repeating: holy smokes.

I liked making lefse once I figured out how to perform the task. That was one of the assignments that worked with Jason's schedule, so we got to do these events together, and all the parents seemed to be in a good mood at lefse-making. I thought I would stroll in and be the best lefse dough roller they'd ever seen. After all, I make my own pie crust—quite successfully—and rolling lefse looked just like it.

Sadly, and much to my frustration and internal embarrassment, I was absolutely not the best lefse dough roller they'd ever seen. I may have even thrown the rolling pin—just a little bit. I blame the dough. Once Jason and I switched jobs and I went on griddle duty, we were cranking out lefse left and right.

One parent job I truly enjoyed was driving the kids to their performances. Imagine a funeral caravan, but instead of a line of cars adorned with black flags, this line of cars was adorned with bright red Norwegian Dancer flags. And the car occupants weren't grieving family members but energetic high schoolers in full bunad costume. Even the girls' hair had to have matching French braids.

Driving these kids gave me my first glimpse into the lives of teenagers. I hadn't been around teenagers since I was one, and I loved listening to them talk, especially Seth, who has always been very driven and focused. On these car rides, I heard them all talk about school, kids at school, their classes, their lives—all the stuff that's important to kids. I kept my trap shut and relished the opportunity for a look behind the curtain. Seth and I also had chances to talk while the other kids were occupied, and it was a great time for us to get to know each other a little bit more and build our bond.

On one of these car rides, we happened to drive by the location of Jason's marriage proposal to me. Seth pointed out to everyone in the car, "Hey, that's where my dad proposed to Tricia." When he shared that with his classmates, my heart nearly burst out of my chest because he sounded proud of that event and wanted to tell others.

Driving the Dancers gave Seth and me an opportunity to get to know each other, and I'm so thankful for that time.

One tradition in this group is a shirt for parents to wear that says "Parent" right on it. Like Tommie, I wanted to be careful not to appear as though I was taking their mom's place. They already had a mom. I supported and helped the family and was happy to do so. And, by this time, I knew that Jason was "the one." Still, I didn't feel right wearing a shirt that declared me as a "Parent." So I requested that one be made without the parent designation, and I wore that one. Now, after a few years in, I would get that Parent shirt and wear the heck out of it.

Through Seth, I got my high school parent experience, and I am so grateful for that opportunity. It was nuts and wonderful at the same time.

You know that ritual between a father and a son when a father gives his son his first beer? StepParents get to do that, too.

I have immensely enjoyed passing things on to my SKids that I got from my parents and StepParents. It's been especially meaningful because I treasure these relationships and am excited to create a legacy from them.

My SMom, Tommie, gave me a sign to hang on the wall that says, "What I am is enough, if I would only be it openly." Tommie knows me. Her presence blesses me, and that sign was a gift from her heart to mine. I placed it right in front of my mirror, where I could see it every day. Sometimes I felt some emotion, a yearning, at the wish to more openly be who I am.

When my SDaughter, Cassie, was moving to a new home, I passed that sign on to her. I can see Cassie, too, yearning to be more open and unsure how to do that. I don't know if she displays it or if it has the same meaning for her, but giving that sign to her meant a great deal to me.

I love having these chances to create these legacies, these meaningful moments that pass from StepMother to StepDaughter, who then passes that on to her own StepDaughter. It's very special to me.

I worked for my mom and my StepDad, Marshall, for many years in the business they built together. They were both my bosses, and I learned a great deal from each of them.

One of my earliest lessons from Mom was to nix "you guys" from my vocabulary. That lesson has stuck with me ever since, along with one of my earliest from Marshall: Never go into a meeting without a pen and paper.

Of course, I learned much more than those two tidbits from working for my parents, and I wish I could say I had the same impact on Happy, but that was not the case.

Happy worked for me at The Virtual Foundry for a short time. That was his first job, and unfortunately, he did not have a very good boss. I didn't know how to be a boss yet and didn't want to tell him what to do (which you'll read more about later). It's pretty hard to be someone's boss when you don't want to tell them what to do.

Even so, I got a huge kick out of it—my StepSon working for me after I had worked for my StepDad.

HAPPY

"Tricia cried at the DMV." It's true. I cried. I tried not to, but I couldn't help it. It was just so meaningful for me.

I grew up on a farm, the kind with cows and crops and tractors. The farm had different machinery, from pickup trucks to dump trucks, tractor lawnmowers to combines that cost as much as a house. I spent a lot of time with my dad on these machines, watching him watch the rows of the field to make sure he was planting all the corn in a straight line, backing up the dump truck so it emptied exactly where it was supposed to, driving the hay baler around while my uncle neatly stacked each bale that came out the end.

I loved these machines and started driving them as soon as my parents said it was safe. The bigger the machine, the more I loved driving it. I got this from Dad; he loves driving, too. I drove tractors before I learned how to drive a car, and really, the car was harder.

Dad took me out one night in a Volkswagen Rabbit from the eighties to teach me how to drive a stick shift. He chose the steep driveway of a business located on a highway for the clutch and gas balancing exercise. If you could get up a hill from a complete stop, you had it down.

Well, I did not have it down. The gears ground, the car lurched, and the engine died. Over and over: Restart the car, left foot on the clutch, right foot on the brake, right hand on the shifter knob, move the right foot to the gas and hammer down! Grind, lurch, kill the engine. Try it again. Move the right foot to the gas and press halfway while letting the clutch out halfway. The engine revs, but the car doesn't move. Grind, lurch, kill the engine.

I tried again and again.

In my memory's retelling of the story, I was really frustrated and maybe started crying a little while Dad got even more frustrated. The experience was not fun at the time (and we both remember it to this day), but the lesson took hold. I understood the interplay between clutch and gas and how to get the car to go up a hill, even if the engine had to rev a lot to do it.

I loved driving. My favorite time of year was the harvest when I drove the big white Case tractor alongside the combine as it pulled the crops from the field. The tractor's radio kept me company while I carted load after load of corn or soybeans from the combine to the dump truck. Fall smells and roaring engines filled my senses, and I felt like a partner to my dad and uncle while we all worked in tandem.

Sometimes Dad would use a semi-truck to haul the crops to the buyer. His skills at backing the semi into crazy spaces always amazed me. He drove a semi, not only for farm work but also as a job for many years. I had stars in my eyes for that big rig and always wanted to drive it myself.

The day finally came. In 2001, I took the plunge and got my own CDL (commercial driver's license). In 2006, I worked a few days a week, about ten hours a day, hauling milk in a tanker truck. My route took me right through the area where I grew up, so I often stopped and saw Dad and Tommie on my way home.

Then, one fateful day, Dad and I ended up driving our respective semis on the same day, on the same highway at the same general time. We knew it was happening, and he pulled over to wait for me to get into the area. Over the CB radio, I told him I was close. He pulled out on the highway, and there we were, father and daughter, driving semis together down the highway, chatting away on the CB.

It was a wonderful, emotional, and proud moment for me, and I'm confident it was for Dad, too. It was the ultimate culmination of this love of driving that we shared. It was my life's driving highlight.

Until Happy passed his driver's test.

This driving bond that my dad and I share was something I'd always wanted to pass on to my own kids. It's been so special to me, and a part of me was a little sad that my life's path hadn't led me to that place where I could have a driving bond with the next generation.

But then, the day I moved into the Charleston home, a friend offered the use of his two small pickups—one a stick shift and the other an automatic. *Here's my chance to pass on the stick legacy*, I thought.

Happy and I went to pick up the old stick shift truck, and I told him he should drive. He looked at me, surprised.

"Come on. I'll teach you."

Even at Hap's young age, he was already showing signs of being an excellent driver, so I assumed teaching him stick would be a cinch. And it was.

Of course, he ground the gears, lurched the truck, and killed it a few times. "Driving stick is like a dance," I told him. "You just have to coordinate your feet. This one goes down at the same time this one comes up. It's a balance. You'll get a feel for it." Rev the engine, jerk the truck forward, kill the engine. It was all part of the process.

Before long, he was shifting like a pro. I was so proud and happy that I could teach him that. Here I was, sharing my driving skills with my StepSon, creating that forever memory like the ones I shared with my dad.

Now there we were at the DMV—just the two of us. I had helped him learn more about the nuances of driving—always so pleased to be able to further this driving bond. Happy passed his driving test without much of a problem, and we entered the line for the license photo.

Internally, I started rehearsing my speech about how meaningful this was for me. I really wanted to convey the specialness of this moment—one I thought had passed me by. I knew I would get emotional and felt very vulnerable, but I had to do it. Letting this moment pass would have been far more foolish than shedding a tear at the DMV.

"You know, Happy," I started. "My dad and I have this driving bond. He taught me how to drive stick and everything else, and we even drove semi together on the highway once. It's such a special bond to me and something I always hoped I could have with a child of my own." Here come the waterworks.

"It just means so much to me to be here with you." I was definitely choking up in the license photo line at the DMV.

Hap let out this sound, like the air streaming out of a tire, and looked away. I did not know what that sound meant, so I chose to interpret it as, "Gosh, Tricia, I didn't know you felt that way, and I'm so happy that you're here with me. I, too, am grateful to share a driving bond with you."

Yes, that's definitely what that sound meant.

Later that day, back at home, Jason asked how it went. Happy's first words were, "Tricia cried at the DMV."

I would do it again, too—every time.

It doesn't even matter that he's not my biological son. He's my StepSon, and our driving bond lives just as deeply in my heart.

Now, all of this takes time to develop. None of the kids liked me at first, especially Cassie.

CASSIE

"I don't really like El Rio."

These six little words were the worst I could have uttered. Cassie was already suspicious about this new woman hanging around, and now that woman had just insulted her favorite restaurant. This introduction lunch was not going well.

Cassie had internet-stalked me. She found some blog posts I'd written years before, which impressed me. And I was also glad. I liked those posts and was proud of them. If that was what she found in her search, I was all for it.

Now, there we were, meeting each other for the first time over lunch at her favorite place. And I said—out loud—that I didn't really like it.

Oy.

We were off to a rough start.

Cassie was never outright rude, but I did catch a little side-eye here and there in the beginning. I knew it was never about me, though.

I mean, yes, if I were a jerk, I couldn't have made it into this family. But the scrutiny wasn't about "Tricia Suess." It was about this new woman, what's her deal, and why is she even here. The Charlestons are very protective of each other, so the scrutiny was warranted. I'm glad she was careful. This bunch deserves the best.

Cassie was mid-launch in her life at college and living in apartments most of the time, only home during breaks and other occasions. She was doing her best to care for her brothers and her dad while taking classes and beginning her life. They had everything all set up. It was working.

And now this new lady is prowling around. Even if subconsciously, I imagine Cassie was wondering if she was being replaced. What role would she have if someone else started taking care of everyone? She couldn't even be there to protect her family because she was at college.

The Charlestons rally around each other when trouble comes, and Cassie was in rally mode.

I felt Cassie begin to soften about a year later when the family desperately needed her help. As the manager of our small city's biggest festival, my time was dedicated to festival duties for a couple of weeks in the spring. And I needed major help. Hap had to get to school every morning and needed food at night. (Get this. Kids need to eat EVERY day! It's crazy.)

We asked Cassie to help, and she came to the rescue. She was a godsend. I think she felt it, too. It was obvious that the family still needed her.

Cassie and I have grown to have a wonderful bond as adult women in a family. We support each other, respect and admire each other, and learn from each other. I wish I were more like her in some ways. She's spirited and driven and very funny.

I love my relationship with Cassie, and watching her grow into the woman she is today has been a joy.

While the kids were sizing me up, I treated them respectfully. It helped that Jason also instilled in them the value of respectful behavior. In large part, Jason is the kind of parent I had always hoped I would be if I had kids of my own. Thankfully, we've been well aligned in that regard. So even when the kids were unsure about me, there was always respect between us.

IT'S NOT ABOUT YOU

Get ready, especially if you've been living alone. You're entering an established family, so you're going from one to many in what seems like an instant. Life isn't just about you anymore. You can't take anything personally.

The kids not liking me in the beginning wasn't about me. Secret conversations they had with each other about me were not about me. The kids not really wanting me to be at their grandparents' house with them was also not about me. Everything every other person does is not about me—it's about them.

People have their own situations, and their actions emerge through that filter. If someone tries to stifle your dream, it's about their own insecurities and has nothing to do with you.

Your SKids will do and say things that kids do, but it's never about you. What you choose to think and feel is your own. If you want to build a happy family, you have to understand that other people's "stuff" isn't about you.

If you take what your SKids do and say personally, you'll have a difficult row to hoe. Instead, focus on you and your values. If you value kindness and compassion, treat your SKids with kindness and compassion, even when it isn't reciprocated. Keep your head forward and your feet moving on your own path. You may not get the lovey-dovey relationship you crave initially, but kids know who's there for them. Most importantly, focus on your own thoughts and actions and act with integrity no matter what the people around you are doing.

If you're unsure what your values are, take a few minutes to suss this out. Read through lists of values online and begin to pare them down. Write down ten or so that resonate with you, then pare that list down to five. Reevaluate and see if you can get it to three. Then try them on. Does each value feel right? Ask yourself these two questions: Do I really reflect this value in my daily life? Would other people see and say this about me?

Don't worry if it doesn't feel like it fits right away. You can try another value on. And guess what? Values naturally change over time, and you can always purposefully change them as well.

I used to have the value "respect, always." But I found that philosophy to be a limiter in my thoughts and actions. I surely don't want to be disrespectful—and don't do that. But I also need the freedom to express my displeasure at times, and my "respect, always" value prohibited that for me in some ways.

When you know who you are, the words and actions of others can't throw you off your path. It's easier said than done, for sure. Like everything else you value, it's a daily practice—another item for your self-care routine.

FOSTERING YOUR RELATIONSHIPS

Once you've established relationships with your SKids, it's time to foster that bond. Each kid is different and requires something different from you, so each relationship must develop on its own.

Cassie was an adult when we met, so we formed a more peer-like relationship. I consciously chose to talk to her on a more adult-to-adult level. We shared secrets and talked about work.

Seth was pretty singularly focused from the beginning. He didn't necessarily need a "parent," although he was still in high school when we met. He just needed support. He needed cheerleaders, and it's always been easy to do that for him.

Happy was only thirteen when we met. Since he was younger, we developed more of a parent-child relationship. I'd love to say that I took a nurturing role with Happy, but I didn't feel like a skilled nurturer. I nurtured Happy to the best of my ability.

A major key was just being myself and letting the kids come to me—SO HARD! Why is being ourselves so counterintuitive? We are inclined to do, say, or think what we think others want us to, but that approach backfires every time.

In my first few years with Happy, he was pretty quiet. I could always tell he was super smart, though. He would hang around, not saying anything but listening closely and watching everything that was going on. I had to work hard at being myself in those moments. It was disconcerting having a young teenager watching everything I was doing, especially when I desperately wanted his approval.

In those moments, I had to pause, breathe, and remind myself that the best course of action is always to be myself. If I could be my authentic self and allow Happy to see me, our relationship could start with stability. He shouldn't have to wonder if what he was seeing was real. He should know, good or bad, what I was about. So, I would forget myself, forget about being observed, and charge forward with my full personality on display. So hard! I became more aware of myself, what I was saying, what I was doing. I sharpened up under Happy's watchful eye and became a better person because of it.

I also approached my relationship with Cassie that way. She needed to know the real me in order to feel good about my joining her family. Being guarded with her would likely have created barriers that would have required much more work to break down later on.

Dating, job interviews, and StepParenting are all great places to be yourself. I've even found that the more I am myself with my mom, the deeper our relationship has grown. That was counterintuitive to me, but it has offered multiple blessings. I don't have to keep up pretenses (which uses up a lot of energy), she gets to know me better, space is created for her to be more herself, and I get to know her better. It's been terrific.

If the thought of being yourself puts you into a bit of a panic, that's okay. Scary things are good for us. It just takes practice. As I've learned this skill, I've rolled it out in bits. I tried out a joke in a situation where I may have been buttoned up in the past. I outwardly expressed not liking something where I might have gone along with it before.

You don't have to put your whole self out there all at once if you're not used to it. You can go in phases, but do work at it. Your relationships will be deeper and more rewarding as you get more comfortable expressing your true self.

I learned a lot of this from Tommie. My StepMom, Tommie, is an angel. Fourth in the order of people who married my dad, Tommie has been a wonderful addition to our family. She cares for our dad in a way that alleviates worry. She loves him and does for him, and it's been wonderful and reassuring to watch the two of them together. She's a gentle soul who deserves to be with another gentle soul. Dad and Tommie are like two peas in a pod. Their capacity for visiting over coffee seems boundless, and I love hearing all the latest updates over a delicious home-cooked breakfast.

Tommie's good for our family. She loves us the way I love my StepKids—with her whole heart.

Tommie helped me break up with a boyfriend who wasn't right for me. Tommie helped me quit a job that wasn't right for me. Tommie helped me clean and stage a house for sale when I couldn't. She hardly ever gives me advice except to ask me what I truly want. And then, when I tell her, she cheers for me, no matter what it is. Her hugs are strong and full of love. Her food is plentiful and full of love. Her presence is welcoming and full of love. Tommie is an angel.

Still, I was scared for her to marry my dad when they were early in their relationship. My other StepMothers and I started off well, but our relationships eroded as time passed. "They 'turned' after they got married," was my interpretation of it, deciding that the wedding day was the factor.

My SKids may have felt the same way about me, and I know it wouldn't have been about me, just as my feelings weren't about Tommie. We all want to feel safe, and bringing a new person into the family can feel unsettling, not knowing what's going to happen.

Tommie continued to love our dad gently and let us come to her in our own time. We could see how much they treasured and cared for each other. And as time went on, it was clear she needed to be a part of our family. Tommie makes all of us better.

Eventually, I begged her. "Please marry my dad!" They're so great together. They're gentle with each other, and that's something they'd both been missing for years. I love them together.

Tommie cleans a few houses for work and sometimes cleans my house. Now and then, I ask her to decorate, which means I say things like, "I want representations of nature but no actual nature," and somehow, she nails it. I love coming home after Tommie's been there. She leaves an energy behind that feels as though she has blessed everything there and finely tuned it to harmony. My home feels extra good after Tommie's been there. So even though we're pretty good at keeping a clean house these days, I still love for Tommie to come sometimes and do that blessing thing. It's just her presence.

Tommie's been through some stuff. Even so, you won't hear her speak an ill word of anyone.

Though she's not my parent, she is kind of one. She's like a chosen parent, even though it wasn't me who chose her. I can feel the way she loves and cares about me without her saying anything.

I don't think Tommie did anything special or purposeful when she was beginning to do things with our family. I'm sure nothing about her approach was calculated. That was just her gentle way. She was maybe even a little timid at times. She supported and laughed and cooked and hosted, and little by little, she won all our hearts.

Tommie never pushed. She let us come to her. She went to our events with Dad and arranged the get-togethers. She participated in our family. And she was just there, cheering us on, listening to our stories, encouraging our time with Dad. She let us build a relationship with her rather than trying to bring it about before its time.

Tommie was always herself. I never felt like the person she presented to me was anything other than who she really was. I could trust her.

The scariest part of entering a family is being yourself. But that's the only way the whole thing is going to work.

BRIBES

I'm not ashamed to admit that initially, I used the occasional bribe to get the kids to like me. The effectiveness of this strategy is tricky, though. They might love the bribe, which may not automatically change their feelings about me. But I figured throwing some positive vibes out there wouldn't hurt, right?

I am not talking about handing off cash. I didn't want to become an ATM. I'm talking about setting the kids up with cool things they would like and maybe wouldn't experience if not for me.

I gave Cassie a birthday gift in secret. I didn't think her dad would've necessarily approved, but I did it anyway. It was a handshake gift with a side of "open this in private." She still was not my biggest fan in those days, and I hoped that having a secret together would help us bond. I know she appreciated the gift. And I know my effort contributed to our building a relationship. (She told me years later that her friends commented to her about that gift, telling Cassie that I was really trying and she should give me a chance.) This was all part of creating a foundation, brick by brick.

Coming up with Happy's bribe was easy. I took him to my family farm, where he could ride four-wheelers over acres and acres of land, fish in the pond, swim in the pool, and check out the tractors and animals. I loved growing up on a farm and hoped that Happy would like that space and, in turn, like me.

Another cool thing about the farm was that he got to see where I came from and know my dad, StepMom, brother and sister, and all my nephews. They're quality, generous people, and I was proud to introduce them to Happy.

I think it worked. He ended up loving the farm, and the whole situation made me a little cooler.

So yes, bribes help.

But look. You can't make yourself a chump. You train others how to treat you, including your kids—bio or otherwise. Just as you don't get to be mean and disrespectful to your kids, they don't get to be that with you.

Before Happy could drive, he would text me asking me to pick up something he needed. Mostly, I was happy to do this for him. I knew that, in some cases, I was his best option for getting those things. In other cases, he just wanted a thing and couldn't get it on his own.

The text came through: *Could you get me a Coke on your way home?*

My thrill at knowing these young people and wanting to build relationships with them typically had me answering in the positive, wanting to give them (nearly) anything they asked for.

At the same time, they needed to be respectful of my time and energy. So I replied with something about including "please" with the request: *Ok, but what's the magic word?*

No response. And guess what? I still got the Coke. I was a little mad at myself about it, but I did it. When I handed it to him, I added, "I asked for the magic word, and I didn't get it, but here's your Coke anyway, so I guess that makes me the chump."

Thankfully, the message was received, and Happy always included a *please* with every future request. I say *thankfully* because I honestly don't know how I would have handled it if he hadn't. Would I have had the courage to ignore a please-less request when I desperately wanted Happy to like me? I hope I would have, but I really don't know.

Building relationships can be tricky, especially with teenagers. Nobody respects a pushover. But I also wanted the relationship to be joyful, and I wanted him—and his brother and sister—to know they could rely on me. It felt like a delicate balance at times.

As StepParents, we're playing the long game, and I knew that from the beginning.

This isn't a quick process. You might not see the fruits of your efforts for ten years or more. You may not ever have deep, loving relationships with your SKids. It doesn't matter. Stay the course. Keep improving yourself. Keep being yourself. Don't take anything personally, and be a grown-up. Have I mentioned this isn't about you? Eyes forward and say, "Thank you."

REFLECTION QUESTIONS

- What are three ways that I can create a team mentality in my family?
- What words would I use to describe my relationship with my StepKids? Using those words, how would I then define our relationship?
- What expectations does everyone in my family adhere to? If we don't have family expectations, what expectations can we agree on?
- How do I show my StepKids I love them?
- Do I take personally things that my SKids or others say to or about me? If so, how can I reframe my reaction?
- In what ways can I be more authentic around my family and friends?

Marriage Advice

"What's your best advice for a long and happy marriage?" I was working my way through the transition from single to married and put this question out into the Facebook universe and asked every married couple I could find in person. I was certain I wanted to marry Jason, and at the same time, I was absolutely terrified. This was so new. I'd never even come close to feeling anything like it. Two bits of guidance really stuck with me. As it turns out, they apply to my Step relationships as well.

SAYING THANK YOU

The first piece of advice is to be liberal with your thank-yous. This advice came to me from my friend and coach, Nancy Kalsow. She explained that she and her husband of many years still thank each other for the small things. Jason and I have been pretty good about thank-yous as well.

After a couple of years of living together, we had naturally split our household chores fairly evenly by interest and skill. Jason does the laundry and dishes, and I manage the paperwork, planning, and groceries. We work together on meal planning, and we both cook. Jason's on garbage duty, and I clean the upstairs bathroom.

When the dog was still with us, I managed his care. After he passed, I secretly hoped that Jason wouldn't notice that one of my major chores was gone, and we wouldn't have to reevaluate the split. Thankfully, we've kept things the same, and I still have clean clothes that are actually IN my closet. Nearly daily, I'm amazed at how I can throw a shirt in the hamper, and then it's just magically clean and on a hanger a couple of days later.

We both manage our designated areas, and this system works well for us. Sometimes Jason has to wash a LOT of dishes. When the dog was alive, I sometimes had to clean out its backside. It all evens out.

So why would I need to thank him for washing the dishes when that's his job? Why should he thank me for getting groceries when it's easy for me, and I do it all on the app? Because it feels nice when your partner thanks you for doing those things. It means they notice and appreciate it. Saying thank you shows you're not taking them for granted. Try it and see what happens.

I'll admit, in the past, in a weird, backward way, I was reluctant to thank Jason for certain things, like how hard he worked. My jumbled thought process was that if I thanked him, I would be acknowledging it, and he might get mad because he worked many more hours than I did. But I tried it for the first time when he told me about a particularly trying day. "Thank you for working so hard for us." It felt good to say it and openly acknowledge the work he puts in to provide for his family. It turns out that thanking him for this was definitely the right thing to do.

He's said the same thing to me a time or two, and let me tell you, it's always great to hear. That appreciation, that simple thank you—especially after a hard day—contributes to feelings of security and partnership. We're saying, "We're in this together. We each have things we're doing and see the contribution the other is making, and we're so glad they are. Thank you."

After practicing saying "thank you" to your spouse, try it with your kids. Happy has to mow the lawn, but a quick, "Hey, the lawn looks really nice. Thank you for doing that," goes a long way. Kids see your example. Happy has even gotten into the thanking habit himself. I haven't come across a situation yet where a sincere "thank you" didn't contribute positively to another person or situation.

EMBRACING GRATITUDE

You can take that "thank you" a step further and let it inform a general feeling of gratitude within you. Gratitude is my favorite emotion. It brings with it a peaceful calm, a sense that everything is just as it should be. I feel fulfilled when I am in gratitude, and an element of joy is included. All the best stuff rolled into one!

Surprisingly, gratitude can take some practice, especially if you're not used to feeling thankful. Humans are hard-wired to look for danger, to be aware of trouble. When you lean into gratitude, you purposefully set your thoughts on the good things in life, pulling the brain away from those pesky people-eating tigers and poisonous berries.

It's time to upgrade your gratitude practice if you say things like the following:

"It's a beautiful day today, but it's gonna rain tomorrow."

"My husband was home early today, for once."

"I love my new furniture, until the dog wrecks it."

Cut that out, and give yourself space to appreciate the good things in your life without any caveats. Enjoy it. You can feel thankful that your bed is comfortable, that the lights come on when you flip the switch, and that you have clean water that just comes out of multiple faucets in your home whenever you want. Okay, these things are rather significant, but you get the idea. There is always something to be thankful for.

Some days, you might have to make some things up, and that's okay. It's fine to reach for gratitude. That's what practicing is all about.

I am thankful for flying first class. I have never actually flown first class, so I'm making this one up. But guess what? If I really feel what it may be like to fly first class, I get to experience it in my mind. The service, the legroom, being able to lie down in an airplane. I love the thought of that. And if I can experience it in my mind and feel gratitude for how that feels, it's more likely to happen for me in real life.

First, find things to be grateful for, and then find things to be grateful for in your spouse and SKids. An easy practice is to write one gratitude statement about your spouse and each of your SKids daily. You don't have to write it initially; just focus on it for a minute. Writing it down eventually is ideal, though.

When you think, *I am grateful for my husband's sense of humor*, allow yourself some space to really take in the words. Imagine your husband cracking a joke that keeps you laughing all day. Breathe in that feeling, and let it wash over you. If you're just starting, you might take five seconds to pause and breathe in gratitude while you're in the shower. If you're advanced, you may be meditating in that feeling for thirty minutes. (I am not advanced.)

My practice is to write statements of gratitude most weekday mornings: • I am thankful for Jason's loyalty.

- I am thankful for Jason's mouth trumpet. (He makes this sound with his mouth like a trumpet, and he trumpets sports channel theme songs, rock hits from the eighties, Christmas carols, and more! If there's a trumpet, that means Jason's happy. I love that trumpet sound.)
- I am thankful for the way Happy maintains the lawn.
- I am thankful for Cassie's help with vacation planning.
- I am thankful for Seth's humor.
- I am thankful for my relationships with my SKids.
- I am thankful for a peaceful, happy home. (I write this one down every day.)
- I am thankful for a humor-filled life.

Gratitude comes in all sizes. It doesn't have to be complicated or time-consuming. Small, consistent effort is the key to gratitude—and everything in life, really—but that's another book. (Look for recommendations in the appendix.)

Gratitude is directed outward. You can send it to God or the Buddha or Jimmy down the street. It's not the recipient of the gratitude that makes the difference; it's the act of being thankful.

The following suggestions can help you develop the habit of embracing gratitude: Set an alarm to help you remember. Put a gratitude statement on your phone screen. Stick a reminder Post-it on your bedroom mirror. Give yourself some grace and space, and surround yourself with gratitude. Your relationships will be deeper and more rewarding if you let this practice develop.

Pause your reading right now and think of one to five things you are grateful for. If you're having trouble coming up with anything, offer a word of thanks that your heart is beating, that your lungs are moving oxygen through your body, that possibility exists in your life.

ASKING FOR FORGIVENESS

The second piece of marriage advice that stuck with me came to me from my childhood friend Andrea. Ask for forgiveness and be forgiving. At first, I wasn't sure what would need to be forgiven within a marriage. Forgiveness seems to carry a weight that indicates egregious infractions. What are married people doing to each other that requires forgiveness?

Then, one day, I told Jason in various ways all the things he was doing wrong: It took not one but two fishing attempts for me to get sympathy from him after I had been stung by a bee. The water he grabbed for me was the wrong brand. The cooler that I made no effort to clean or care for wasn't up to my cleanliness standards. And all of that was after I had unceremoniously "asked" him to run my errands for me.

Jeez, can this guy catch a break?

Yes, indeed, forgiveness plays a role in a marriage and all relationships.

It's important to recognize your own failures and ask your partner to accept and love you. In this context, when you ask for forgiveness, you're asking for your partner to help you be better. You're asking for the two of you to move forward together. "How can we make this right? What can we do to keep this from happening again?" It's a partnership—one person is never one hundred percent at fault—

so when one of you messes up, it's up to both of you to fix it and move forward.

When I was in the throes of managing our city's festival, I asked Jason to pick up a piece of jewelry for my costume from a local store, and he forgot. It was not on his radar. He didn't understand the urgency because I didn't communicate how important it was to me.

I registered the kids for school and paid too much of Jason's money because I handled it my way rather than how he would have. I needed to honor his request, and he needed to communicate the importance of handling his money in that way.

These were the foibles of a new relationship—figuring out what was important to each other by messing stuff up.

We apologize, recognize that we both play a part, talk it out, and move on. (Although I suspect that when Jason reads this, he'll give me a ribbing with the ol' "We're still talking about that jewelry?")

A forgiveness practice becomes even more important with kids. They don't have the depth of experience to understand human failings. It's up to us to model forgiveness by showing how to forgive each other in a family and how to forgive others to maintain our sense of peace.

Kids make SO MANY mistakes on their way to adulthood. (Although adults make plenty of mistakes, too.) They're figuring out how to be in this world, and it's important that they're shown how to protect their peace when harmed and make amends when they cause harm. Messing up is a big part of the human experience, and you can't escape it. But you can learn to manage those occasions with grace.

When you forgive within your family, you're saying that you understand the humanness in one another and that people mess up. You're saying that you still accept and love them and want to figure out how to move forward together by rebuilding the team and investing in the family unit.

You're also saying that you don't want to carry the burden of resentment within yourself. You choose, quite purposefully, to leave that infraction in the past. You don't have to forget it, but it no longer needs to be a festering part of you. It's never used as fuel in an argument. Rather, it's laid to rest because, in the grand scheme of things, it doesn't matter.

When you ask forgiveness, you recognize that you could have done better, whether or not you knew that at the time. You're acknowledging your failing—your humanness—and declaring that you want to continue trying to improve.

These acknowledgments aren't weakness. It's not a disadvantage to own your error. Rather, when you can admit your failing and commit to doing better, you show strength of character and mind. Truly accepting yourself as a regular person who messes up sometimes offers emotional freedom. You don't have to be perfect. In fact, you *can't* be perfect. You're human; it's not allowed. What does perfect even mean, anyway?

It would be great if you could periodically strengthen yourself without going through the messing-up part first. Yet, people tend to let things slide and settle into a status quo until there's some shake-up that causes you to pause (and hopefully breathe) and think and assess. What's the next step? Build. Take each other's hands and take the next step forward together.

WATCHING YOUR WORDS

Words matter a great deal, especially words passed from an adult to a child. If you're a StepParent, your StepKids have been through some stuff. They might be jaded and skeptical. They could be comfortable and happy on the outside, but they're likely still hurting. Even though you're not their parent, your words make a huge difference.

Your StepKids might act out. They might snap at you or act rudely toward you. Whatever they do, it is never your place to disparage them. That's not to say you need to accept disrespectful behavior, but you do need to be the adult and remember that it's not about you. If their pain is spilling out onto you, help them with it rather than reacting to the symptoms of it.

Parenting and StepParenting are challenging. Here's this kiddo you're sharing a house with, you're sharing a person with, and they probably won't behave as you think they should. (I mean, who does, really?) You're probably not behaving the way they think you should, either. You might feel impotent, like you're in an impossible situation. You're trying to love them, and they want none of it. They might not talk to you. They might not listen to you. None of that matters. You're the adult—you need to act like one.

It is never okay to tell a kid they're bad or lazy or fat or an inconvenience or anything else like that. You don't get to label those kids. If you love your spouse, you need to love their kids. And that might mean loving them while disliking them. That might mean loving them while they do the opposite of what they're supposed to be doing. Love them anyway, and use loving words with them. Patience is key. This, too, shall pass.

When you're wounded, gathering the energy for patience and tolerance is that much harder. Holding back your angry words is much harder when you're in pain, making it hard to pass peace along. Be in charge of yourself, and if you're not, work on it. Get some therapy, hire a life coach, or do some journaling.

Do whatever it takes to make yourself whole so you can give your entire self to your family. But what does it mean to make yourself whole? It means that you know and accept yourself—all of you. Feeling unworthy of love, peace, joy, or a happy family is normal. But if you fill those internal holes with love for yourself, you'll be able to love those around you. No one else can do the work for you, and you owe it to those you share a life with—and to yourself.

How you treat yourself, how you feel about yourself, and how you judge yourself will be how you treat, feel about, and judge those around you. What words do you tell yourself? Do they encourage you and lift you up? Or do they make you feel shitty and guilty and shameful? You choose the words you say to yourself and the feelings they generate.

Besides not making you feel great, angry words have a devastating effect on kids—it doesn't matter that you're not their parent. You're a kind-of parent. At the least, you're an adult who lives in the same house. Your words matter. When you label your Steps, they'll wear those labels into adulthood. Lazy, fat, unwanted, unnecessary. Don't do that to another person. If you want to label your Steps, choose labels like capable, smart, and earnest.

RESPECTING YOUR STEPKIDS' OTHER PARENT

Your word choice is also critical when talking about your SKids' other parent. One fundamental lesson I learned from all of my parents that I've carried forward into my own StepParenting experience is respect for your StepKids' other parent. This extends to Steps referencing the other parent, parents referencing the other parent, and even spouses referencing each other. There's no room for disrespect in any of these relationships.

I know that people do shitty things to each other, and it can be hard to hold back your vitriol. Again, it isn't about you. It isn't about how you feel about what went on between your spouse and their ex. It's about your SKids and their need to feel secure and loved by all their parents, including you.

Children of divorce need to go through a process of figuring out how to love their parent and their StepParent at the same time. It can feel like a betrayal to their parent to also love their Step. As adults, we know it's possible to love many people because each relationship is different. Kids don't have that depth yet. They only know a few ways to be in relationships, which are modeled by parents, grandparents, aunts and uncles, teachers, and friends. This StepParent business is a whole new ball of wax, and kids need time to figure that out.

Your StepKids, especially if they're younger, want to love you. They want to view you as another kind of parent. They want to have fun with you, watch movies with you, and get help with their homework. They want to look up to you.

So from a kid's perspective, it's confusing if you use pejorative language about their other parent. Here's one person they love and respect saying bad things about another person they love and respect. At the least, it causes them to question who is right. At the worst, it makes you look bad because they know their parent more than they know you. Chances are, they'll defend their parent—at least with their feelings—and apply distance to their relationship with you. If your criticism of their parent creates a wedge, that is on you, StepParent.

Even if the other parent is a complete jerk, there is no room in a loving relationship for you ever to express that to your SKid. You're talking about their mom or their dad. Imagine someone saying those same things about your mom or dad. That hurts. You would not like it, and it would color how you view the person saying it. Don't do it to your Steps.

You probably want to talk about the other parent and also may need to. These are tricky relationships. That's what friends and confidential conversations are for. Express those feelings away from the home and away from any accidental listeners. Be careful about sharing criticisms with your spouse as well. Your spouse loved that person, at least for a time. When you criticize their ex, you're criticizing their choice, which doesn't feel good for anyone either. It's easy to let feelings of jealousy and defensiveness creep in. That's okay. Just be very mindful of how you act upon those feelings.

A NOTE TO PARENTS: The same advice applies to you. When you use critical language about your ex in front of your kids, it is very confusing for the kids. Someone they love and respect is saying mean things about someone else they love and respect, and they don't have the experience to defend their other parent or to recognize that this is an issue between adults. It's very personal for them. Let your kids freely love their other parent without your interference. If that person is not so awesome, your kids will figure it out on their own.

Imagine life as a kid where everything is going along fine. Or maybe it's not fine because your parents fight, but at least you know they both love you. Then one of them moves out, and your world dramatically changes, and you have no control over it. Now you have to figure out what this new situation is. If you still know that both of your parents love you—from separate houses now—you're okay. This new setup is going to work.

Then a new adult is introduced as your parent's "friend," and you wonder what the heck is happening. But they seem nice, so you give them a chance. Time goes on, and the new friend is around a lot more. You get to know them. They're kind to you and may do things differently than your parent, but it's not too bad.

Your parents speak well of each other, allowing you to love them freely, just as you have been. And the new friend who now lives in your house also speaks well of your other parent. It's a little weird at first, but you figure out how to love this new person, too.

The bonus that makes this new person okay is that your other parent approves. They told you explicitly that it's okay to love the new person, and it's okay for your parent and the new person to be together. Your other parent tells you they're glad your parent is happy. We're off to the races now! Now you have permission from all three to love the others freely. There's no confusion, no defending required, no question. You are loved. You are secure. You are in an excellent position to thrive.

Now, what happens when your mom makes an off-handed remark about your dad? Ouch. There's a little step backward. And maybe your dad doesn't think it's so great that your mom has a new friend, and he talks about it to you or in front of you. There's another step backward. And when the StepParent says the other parent is doing things all wrong, what are you supposed to think now?

Rather than having permission to love all three freely, you must navigate this new temperamental situation. Rather than devoting your energy to thriving, some of it needs to be set aside for maneuvering around your parents' feelings about each other and figuring out how you feel about them all. And because they're saying untoward things about each other, you may start to wonder a little bit if they love you, which makes you feel unsteady! Instead of being set up to thrive, you're being taught to manipulate and disrespect others. You're being shown that vitriol is okay no matter where it lands or who it hurts.

It's not hard to be respectful. It starts with the understanding that no one is perfect (including you, friend) and that we are never free from responsibility for our life's situations. At the least, save your venting for private. Set your kids up for success by assuring them that they are loved and that they have permission to love all of their parents freely.

ASKING FOR WHAT YOU NEED

Though I do slip occasionally, I don't tell my SKids what to do. I had a challenging relationship with my first StepMother. She told me what to do SO MUCH, and it did not feel good. When I entered these relationships with my SKids, I desperately did not want to tell others what to do, so much so that I took it a little bit too far. I still needed to be an adult living in a house with kids. When living with others, it's okay to have expectations about how to live together in a household.

I ran everything through Jason to avoid telling anyone what to do: "Jason, can the kids not leave the living room lights on and TV at full volume when they go to bed?"

I would talk to Jason about it, and then he would share the message that we need to turn stuff off when we go to bed. Bleh! It felt like the chicken's route. I did not like communicating through an intermediary, but that's where my fear and courage had me at that point.

That's an area I could have approached more confidently, but I was reluctant to tell others what to do. I couldn't even ask for help. "Would you please ...?" or, "When you have time, could you ...?" I wasn't even willing to do that much.

I previously mentioned that I was not a good boss for Happy when he worked for me. Can you imagine working for someone who never told you specifically what to do and only barely asked you to do things? What chance do you have for success?

Happy was a trooper. He tried but didn't have the right tools for the job and had to make it up since he wasn't given much direction. I tried to manage through ESP, and that did not work. I couldn't even fire him in person. I did it by text and felt like a big chicken for doing so. *Man, I'm the grown-up here. I should be doing this in a grown-up way.* Happy's employment was a valuable lesson for me.

It took me a while until I felt secure enough in the relationships to be able to ask for help or to ask for a chore to be done. Running everything through Jason was inefficient and felt like a telling-my-friend-to-tell-my-other-friend situation. I knew I could do better.

While I wish I could have been more direct, it worked out fine. We're all figuring it out as we go. Happy is the only SKid still living at home, and I'm okay with asking for his help when I need it now, although I still try not to do that very often.

REFLECTION QUESTIONS

- How do I thank the ones I love for everything they do?
- Is it time to upgrade my gratitude practice? What are five things I am grateful for today?
- Can I practice gratitude in my daily life through writing, meditation, or some other means?
- Am I able to forgive others I love (including myself), or do I hold on to their past mistakes?
- How do I speak to the people in my life? Do I label or judge the people I love?
- Am I careful with my words when I talk about my SKids' other parent?

Establishing a Parenting Agreement

THE DISCIPLINARIAN

I was caught. My sister knew what I was up to and accidentally spilled the beans to Marshall. I wanted to be mad at her, but her snitch was entirely an accident (she was a dry snitch, in the vernacular). And there I was, sitting on the other side of Marshall's desk, finding out that he found me out. I had lied about where I was.

Marshall told me this was my one allowed mistake. He wouldn't tell my mom and vowed to keep my secret. But this was a one-time-only offer. I had better not find myself on this side of the desk having this conversation again. That situation confirmed, once again, Marshall's character and caring nature.

Mom dated a couple of people after she divorced. One of them chewed tobacco and had horses that I could ride and these sweet yellow cowboy boots that I still think about. I remember always liking that man. The other man I remember had two sons around my age, and they had an Atari—my first exposure to Pong.

But the man who finally stole her heart was Marshall. They met at a tax seminar where Marshall was speaking. Mom approached the podium to ask a question after the presentation ended, and the rest is history.

Marshall lived in a small apartment near a rough neighborhood. I can still see my mom in that little apartment, doling sums of cash into envelopes—her method of budgeting. I've watched all of my parents handle money with great skill, and these cash envelopes were my first blatant lesson. When the cash in the envelope ran out, that was it. No more groceries or clothes or whatever the envelope said on it.

Their financial acumen makes sense. Marshall was involved with a tax preparation company in the city, and my mom's family had tax practices where they lived—and still do. I helped Marshall from time to time in the tax office, which would become a recurring activity until my last stint at the ripe old age of forty-four.

As a girl, I loved helping my dad in his farm office. I got to stuff the envelopes, lick them shut, and place the stamps for all the bills he was paying. As a young teen, I was also happy to help Marshall in his office. One particular assignment was to tear perforated checks apart. I knew about tearing checks in half to void them but not tearing them apart at the perforation. So I ripped them in half with glee. *Riiiiiippppp!*

I probably ripped up twenty or thirty checks before Marshall came in to find out what the sound was. He laughed when he saw what I was doing, understanding that I was simply following the direction to tear the checks apart. Having never seen checks like that, I did what I thought I should.

I remember this story fondly because Marshall was kind about it. I was messing up, destroying a bunch of checks, but he just laughed with me about the misunderstanding.

Mom moved to Wisconsin to be with him, and I followed after graduating high school. I lived with Mom and Marshall while I attended college classes. By then, they lived in a house in a small town and made a room for me in the basement.

All the while, Marshall worked—a lot. He left before sunrise and came home in the wee hours of the morning. I messed up a few times, as young adults do when figuring out how to be adults. Marshall was never a part of that, though. Whenever I was in trouble, it was with Mom. There was the ol' "Mom sitting in the dark" in the living room while I tried to sneak the boy out of the basement. You know bad things are going to happen when you come upon your parents sitting in the dark.

Marshall wasn't a part of that because that was their policy with each other—they would not discipline the other's kids. They wouldn't tell the other's kids what to do or try to parent them. This was a great arrangement. I'm sure there were private conversations where they discussed what to do about a particular situation. But the calls to the boy's house to tell me to come right now, the sitting in the living room in the dark, the check-in of grades was all Mom. Though sometimes Marshall would offer moral support, that was their agreement.

We were in a blended family. I had StepBrothers (I still do), and Mom and Marshall fully abided by their discipline agreement. If something was going down, they were responsible for their own kids.

The policies that Mom and Marshall had served as an example for Jason and me. I knew about their rule of not disciplining the other's kids and shared that with Jason. We both agreed this policy was worth adopting for ourselves. The discipline agreement provided the major point in our Parenting Agreement, a critical contract between parents. If a Parenting Agreement is not discussed and created intentionally, it will still develop but by happenstance.

Jason is a great parent. He's the kind of parent I hope I would have been had I had kids of my own. He respects his kids as people, and they return that respect. He guides them and trusts them to make their own decisions.

Jason and I have definitely had different ideas about certain aspects of life for the kids. He asks for my opinion, and I offer it.

(Sometimes I offer it without being asked. That doesn't work so well.) But ultimately, it's still up to him. He never lets things go too far, but we have had differences of opinion over time. He's had to shut me down a couple of times by reminding me that this part of parenting is his job. He loves being a parent and embraces that role, so I bite my tongue and trust him. It's hard, of course, when you know what's best despite never having raised kids yourself and only being around them for a few years.

You may be wondering if I lose my power by not being in a disciplinary role. The answer is no. Again, I'm not their parent—I'm a kind-of parent. My SKids don't need me to discipline them; they need me to love, respect, and support them, to help provide a happy and stable home. If I do those things and ensure that I am respected in the process, I have all the power I need. We make this home together.

Ultimately, the kids are wonderful people who've grown up to be well-adjusted, high-contributing adults. The proof is in the pudding, though going through it was still nerve-wracking at times.

Everybody needs to know what roles they will play in different situations. Some families may come together, and the StepParent wants to take on the role of disciplinarian, or the parents will share some of that. Some of these things come into play more when the kids are little. My SKids were at least teenagers and almost young adults when I came along, so it would not have been appropriate for me to come in and start doling out discipline, telling them what to do and running the household or trying to run their lives as an extension of that.

Though Jason and I had intentionally established our discipline rule, the rest of the stuff in our agreement developed on its own. It likely would have been helpful for us to consider more points and add those to our agreement, but we didn't have a book like this guiding us!

OTHER PARENTAL ROLES

In addition to the importance of disciplinary roles in keeping clear expectations for the kids and you, other roles should be considered when sorting out your Parenting Agreement. Kids have full lives and their own stuff going on and need help with it all.

Below are factors to consider when creating your Parenting Agreement:

- Who makes healthcare decisions and healthcare appointments?
- Who attends parent-teacher conferences?
- Who decides on and signs the kids up for sports, orchestra, chess club, and other extracurriculars?
- Who makes the decisions on religious activities?
- Who helps with body hygiene, like ensuring pre-teens are wearing deodorant and assisting girls in managing their period?
- Who is in charge of routines, like getting up for school, brushing teeth, doing homework, and taking out the trash?
- Who is in charge of discipline, like punishments for breaking curfew or putting a mystery dent in the car, and *no one* knows how it got there?
- How about those "you only get one" major mess-ups (I really mean the stronger, impolite word there) that each of us does and your SKid will inevitably do?

It's important to get all of your issues straightened out ahead of time. Your daily life and that of your SKids will flow more easily when the roles are defined. They'll have a better understanding of rules and boundaries when they're coming from one person.

WHERE I FELL SHORT

While I'm proud of the way I approached these relationships, there are some things I would do differently if I could go back and do it again. I knew going in that each kid would need an individualized relationship. And I sure tried. But I wasn't perfect. I fell short in many ways.

Primarily, I wish I had been more nurturing with Happy. I lacked the courage to express more affection and care with him, hug him more, care for him when he was sick, and be that motherly figure in our home.

I can—and did—check all the basic care boxes. But I have a bit of sorrow about not being more ... motherly, I guess. I always felt guilty whenever I wanted to hug Hap and then didn't because I was scared of being too much. I always wanted to give him space, and I gave him so much that I worry he missed out on much of the love and care he deserved.

I don't know. Maybe it was perfect for him. I never actually asked. When Happy reads this, it will be the first he learns of it, so here goes ...

Happy, I'm sorry I didn't hug you more. I'm sorry I didn't give you a more motherly presence in our house. I'm sorry I didn't attend to you better when you were sick. I wish I had reached out more.

REFLECTION QUESTIONS

- Do we agree on who disciplines the kids and how to discipline them? If not, what are our values around discipline and its role in our family?
- How could a parenting agreement benefit our family? What items should be included?
- Can I identify our specific roles in our marriage and as parents? If not, identify our roles and consider building a parenting agreement around them.

PART THREE
US

Making a Family

"What's that sound? Oh, shit. It's the smoke alarm." We were out back, getting the grill ready to start on the evening meal, when we heard the telltale shrill *BEEP BEEP BEEP* of the smoke alarm going off in the kitchen.

It won't be a big deal. We were cooking and sometimes that happens. We'll just open a window, shift a pan around or something, and it'll be fine.

It was only my second week living with the Charlestons, and I had set a cloth oven mitt on the back burner of the stove (which is against one of my rules: do not put flammable things on the stove at any time, ever), and turned on the front burner. Except I didn't turn on the front burner; I turned on the back burner and then walked out of the house.

So we strolled into a kitchen FULL of smoke. This wasn't like when you overcook bacon or leave cookies in the oven a little too long. This was the thick, can't really breathe in it, type of smoke. I was about as alarmed as the actual alarm.

That oven mitt was sending a thick plume of smoke into the air. Surely it would have burst into flames at any second! *BEEP BEEP BEEP*

We sprang into action. I opened every window and door in the kitchen and living room while Jason somehow grabbed the mitt and tossed it into the sink, immediately running water on it. I'm sure there was a lot of swearing.

I turned off the burner, and then *BEEP BEEP BEEP* we both knocked that *BEEP BEEP BEEP* smoke alarm off the wall to get it to stop.

But then we had to get out. The smoke was overwhelming. We'd go back in for a few seconds at a time to make sure the mitt was out and try to move more smoke through, and then we'd have to get back outside. I had never been in smoke that thick. My childhood fire training ran through my mind: "Stop, drop, and roll." *Okay, no, I'm not on fire. I don't need to do that.* And then more training: "Stay low under the smoke." Yeah, that one made sense.

Neither of us actually got low, but we did not stay in that kitchen very long. We dashed inside a few more times to monitor the situation and do what we could to move the smoke out as quickly as possible.

Of course, in any "emergency" scenario, lots of possibilities run through your mind. *Is everything smoke-damaged? Are we going to have to get all new stuff? (Would that be so bad?) Are the landlords going to kick us out? Are the Charlestons going to kick ME out?*

Thankfully, none of those scenarios played out. The whole scene calmed down after a bit, and there was no damage to the stove or anything else. The smell went away along with the smoke. The mitt did not make it through the event. Nor did my pride.

"Yeah, hey, Charlestons, living with me is going to be great."

SHARING THE SAME SPACE

No doubt, all of us living together was weird at first. The kids had to have wondered who this lady was and why she was now in their house. For me, I'd been living alone for twenty years—yes, TWENTY years of living alone. I had full control of the remote. No one smelled the weird food I cooked or saw me walking about in various stages of undress. Now I'm in a house with three, sometimes four other people.

It took us all a while to get used to being in the house together. We all had to adjust and make small changes to accommodate each other. The kids needed to stop leaving the TV in the living room on full volume at night when they went to bed. I needed to start dressing appropriately when I left my bedroom.

More seriously, though, I needed to start trusting my new housemates. Hearing other people in the house was new. When the kids had friends over, I got really weird about it. *Who are these people? What are they doing here?* It was very different from the solitary life I'd been used to.

"Jason! I just need to know who's here. Who is in this house with me?"

"It's just Happy's friends. It's normal. It's fine."

"There are sTrAnGeRs in my house!"

"Honey, it's just the kids. It's fine."

Yeah, I was definitely weird about it, but Jason helped me through, just as he always does.

I eventually got used to the friends and got to know who they were. Most of them, anyway. I'll tell you what. When you're not used to interacting with, being around, or even looking at teenagers, they can all look the same.

Think about it. When you, as a whole family, move into a new house, the energy of the previous family might still be there. But it doesn't take long to shift that energy and change the feeling of the place because everyone's taking it over together. You move in all your furniture, quickly start cooking with familiar smells, and hang your art on the walls. You take over the whole space, and it soon becomes yours.

But when you move into a house where a family already lives, you are not only moving into established—and ongoing—energy, you're also entering the family culture. You have to figure out how to navigate that energy and that culture.

What TV shows do they watch? What kinds of meals do they have? Are they into fitness or hunting or board games or old cars? What kind of events do they like to attend? Do they load the toilet paper up (correct) or down (I don't know why anyone would do it this way)? Do they squeeze the toothpaste tube neatly from the bottom and always replace the cap, or do they squeeze it from the middle and can't even find the cap like a bunch of animals?

All those little things about living a regular life differ from family to family, and it was my job as the newcomer to ease in, find out how they do things, adapt to that way, and then begin to add my own flavor to it.

Have you ever gotten a new boss at work? You're going along, everything's fine, and then the news comes out that you're getting a new manager or CEO. It's nerve-wracking because you don't know how it will go. This person will directly impact your daily life at work, and they're coming in here not knowing anything about how you and your team work.

Did that boss come into their office on day one and start making changes? Or did they come into their office on day one and start asking questions? It's easy to see which approach will create trust and cohesion more quickly.

In my case, there wasn't a lot of distance between Jason's divorce and our meeting. So the kids' mom was still kind of in the house: her energy, some of her things, the food she often used for cooking.

But look. That's okay. The kids still needed her to be present. They didn't choose this rodeo; they're along for the ride. My goal was to give them some grace and space (my two favorite things) and respect their experience in the process. Kicking their other parent's energy out was not going to be the first thing I did. I was confident enough in myself and in my relationship with Jason to let the kids' mom have a presence in the house. I knew it would shift over time.

It takes a beat to transition. The name of the game is respect, and kids need to have both parents with them for a while. A lot of changes happened in their young lives in a very short time. I know what it's like when a new person moves in. It felt important to respect their space as it was.

It's easy to think things like, *I'm the grown-up here, and this is my house now*, but it's not, really. It was their house, and I was invited into it. It was my job to respect the existing culture, integrate into it, and then add my influence to it.

Do the right thing. It isn't about you.

Most of the time, doing the right thing benefits you, but even when it doesn't, do it anyway.

Moving in was a big "it's not about me" moment. This was the time to do the right thing, which meant taking things slowly. I *wanted* to change out all the furniture and towels and rugs and art, but I *needed* to take baby steps, build together, and let everything unfold over time. I needed to let the way I lived interact with the way the Charlestons lived, find commonalities, come together where we were different, and learn how to live together.

As time and relationships progressed, as we began to build our own new culture together, we could start to shift. This slow pace gave the kids time to see their other parent in their new space. It gave everyone time to settle into the new ways of things.

They could participate with me in that space. With my energy established there, it got a little easier. That's when I felt okay with moving more into the space, putting my stamp on it, making it the new "ours."

It's not always the case where there's so little time between the previous spouse and you. It may be different when the person you're dating has been divorced for a while, and the previous spouse has been absent from the house. In this case, you're not transitioning energy but focusing more on establishing your new group energy.

But the same principle applies. You need to observe the family culture and then integrate into it. By the time you've moved in, you've likely spent significant time with this new family, so you understand how they operate. Living in the same house is another level to navigate.

I was not moving into a place that was now my house. It had to be "our" house. So I made it a slow transition, always keeping in mind that it wasn't just about me. At the same time, I lived there as a whole person, and it also needed to be my home.

The Charleston house I moved into was aggressively tan. Tan walls, tan furniture, tan towels. The house I moved out of looked like a rainbow exploded in it. I fretted a bit about the absence of color in this new place and how I could get more color without completely disrupting the vibe. Does this family even like colors?

My lime green couch and orange chairs eventually made their way into the living room. My multi-colored bath towels were put into rotation. And my colorful kitchen spoons ended up in a big bright orange crock right where I could see them. I felt more confident that this was going to work.

THE KITCHEN

The kitchen was another story. It's one thing to install your energy into your bedroom and hangout spaces. The kitchen took quite a bit more time for me. Many of the foods the kids' mom used for cooking were still there. Plus, I was an insecure cook. Living alone, I made weird food that I assumed only I would like. I was nervous about cooking for others because I didn't think anyone else would like what I had made. So I didn't make anything.

I knew I could find recipes online, and I had several cookbooks. But I didn't know what kids, especially teenagers, liked to eat. There was so much fast food for the first couple of years. I felt kind of bad feeding these children Arby's and Taco Bell a couple of times a week. I'm a woman. Aren't I supposed to naturally know how to feed children? Don't ovaries give you special magic food prep powers? Indeed, they do not. I would be fine with popcorn and ice cream for supper every night. So, we all ate like old-timey bachelors. Besides all the fast food, there were a lot of chicken patties and tater tots, tacos and spaghetti—real easy stuff.

But over time, I started experimenting in the kitchen. I actually put some of those chicken patties and tater tots in the oven. Hey, I'm cooking! Then about a year in, I did an overhaul. I threw out everything expired, rearranged the snack cupboard, and set up all my spices near the stove. Now it was time to cook.

I got used to making things everyone would like, which, at that time, meant there could be nothing green. I remembered that I could make excellent chili and put that into the meal rotation. We started grilling out a bit. Over time, the tater tots turned into actual potatoes, which eventually turned into vegetables, and the chicken patties turned into chicken breasts, beautifully seasoned and grilled to perfection.

THE LAUNDRY

It took a couple of years for the energy of the house to shift, to include me in that shift, and to understand how we were going to be together as a family there. We settled into our grooves, created our own spaces, and put our towels into our own laundry baskets.

Jason and I don't do the laundry for the entire household because I won't do it for a person who can do it on their own. I did my own laundry as a kid, and Jason's philosophy has been to transfer laundry duties to the kid the first time they complain that something wasn't done or wasn't done right.

I do have to contradict myself here since Jason does all my laundry, and thank goodness he does because if I were left to my own laundry devices, I would be getting dressed in front of the dryer every morning. I use the pile system to manage my clothes. I make sure to never complain about any part of the laundry because I do not want to do it myself. I'm so thankful he does that.

"Jeez, why is Mom so uptight about these towels?"

My mom was always on my sisters and me about the bath towels. We always had to hang them up EVERY time we used them. It's just a wet towel. Who cares.

Well, Mom cared. I didn't get it then, but I fully understand it now.

A wet towel on the floor is a grand offense. It just sits there with its moisture-breeding bacteria, painting mildew on every surface it touches, creating a stench that might not come out. When I look at a wet towel on the floor, I can almost see it moving with everything happening in there.

Public Service Announcement: Towels need to dry out!!

The Charleston kids, just like me as a kid, just like every other kid probably in the world, didn't seem to understand how moisture works. They piled up their towels in the corner of the bathroom. IN THE CORNER! That's even worse.

I'm pretty sure each of us thought someone else would pick them up and wash them. But no one did that. I sure wasn't going to. I was the least domestic person I knew. As you now know, I usually had popcorn for supper and had to have someone else clean my 800-square-foot apartment. It wasn't going to be me handling those towels. So they just stayed there, the pile growing.

Something had to be done. Picking up wet towels may have been the first household request I made of the kids via text because there was no way that I could've said it directly to everyone at that point in our relationship.

The text said something about everyone being in charge of their own towels: *We can't have wet towels on the floor—they're creating mildew on the walls. Just put it in your own laundry when you're done with it.*

It was a scary moment for "Dad's girlfriend" to make the big declaration about wet towels. But it had to be done. Apparently, that was the first stand I felt strongly enough to make.

My mother would be proud.

ACCEPTING YOUR FAMILY'S CULTURE

This business about the wet towels represents the larger picture of figuring out how to live with people who have been doing things differently from you this whole time. I used to think everyone did everything the same in their households, like the one I grew up in. One morning, I came face-to-face with this non-reality when I was at a friend's house, and the kids started putting chocolate chips and peanut butter on their pancakes.

Excuse me. What is this now? That is not how you eat pancakes. You put syrup on them. Maybe some butter, but definitely syrup and absolutely nothing else. Chocolate chips and peanut butter? That's madness.

It's madness *and* a great example of different family cultures. It had never once occurred to me to put anything other than butter and syrup on a pancake. But that was totally normal for my friend's family.

What might be normal in the Charleston household that didn't exist in mine? And how do we mix those two styles together? I had to accept that they probably did some things differently. Since I didn't have kids in my house before, I was going to learn about a lot of new and different aspects of daily life. There were also several Charlestons and only one of me, so I knew I would be outnumbered in anything I thought was "not normal," like how one eats a pancake.

This is where the "observation then integration" plan becomes key. It's okay that other people put weird shit on their pancakes. It's not wrong; it's just another way of doing a thing. There are about a million different ways of doing things, and just because I learned a certain way, that doesn't make it correct and true for everyone. (Loading the dishwasher, anyone?)

Different people do things differently. As the incoming Step, your job is to chill out about it. Let them do those things differently than you did. It's small potatoes. It doesn't matter in the grand scheme of things that there now needs to be pasta every time there's chili. Big whoop. Just make the pasta.

Here's my advice on this topic:

- Keep your toothpaste separate if you don't like how other people handle the tube.
- Let go of your need for the toilet paper to be installed one way or the other.

You're going for a happy home, not one where everyone does everything the way *you* think it should be done. "Happy and peaceful" are far more important than "right."

Now the house is fully "ours." We have personalized our spaces, hung our pictures, cooked our food, and established our new family culture.

As a team, we support each other, cheer for each other, roast each other, and love being together. We each bring a full personality, and nobody's sitting quietly in the corner. Sometimes I have to grab for my place in the conversation. Sometimes I get the floor and have a rapt audience, ready to laugh, cheer, or roast whatever I say. It's such a fun group.

We even have a motto: "Get after it!" We're all out there, getting after it, whatever "it" may be.

And if we're not living up to our potential or doing quite the right thing, Jason will let us know by "going Dad" on us. Going Dad means that Jason is going to tell you where you're falling short. With kindness and respect, he'll let you know that what's happening is not what should be happening. It often includes a "Be better" at the end, but that depends on the situation.

He's kind and firm in his delivery, and you feel perhaps embarrassed at first because you're being shown yourself, perhaps contrite or even disappointed with yourself. But by the end, you're inspired to indeed be better.

I was once on the receiving end of this lecture-like speech about how what was happening wasn't right, and I did not like it at first. But Jason wasn't wrong. I was feeling undeserving of something, and he told me, in no uncertain terms, that I deserved it and needed to take advantage of the opportunity. This particular occasion didn't end with a "Be better" but rather a message to demand more for myself. And he was right. I took his words to heart and did demand more for myself.

I'll say he's always right when he "goes Dad." This most Daddest part of him comes out when some injustice is happening that needs to be corrected. The pizza guy gave our pizza to a random person in a car across the street. C'mon, man. Be better. A friend crossed one too many boundaries. You gotta be better. Or someone he loves isn't living up to their potential. You deserve more.

(I sometimes wonder how Jason's Dadness affected that pizza guy. Is it something he'll remember forever, or just another interaction with another customer? I like to think it's the former, and since I'll never know, I'm sticking with that.)

Jason is the anchor for all of us. He provides a steady platform from which we can all launch and really find out what we're capable of. He is the glue that holds us all together.

I count my lucky stars every day that I get to be in this awesome family. And while luck has played a huge role, I have also put in a lot of work. Magical, happy families don't just happen. They need to be fostered and nurtured, with each person doing their part.

ROWING TOWARD YOUR GOALS

Picture yourself on the shore of the ocean. Your view is massive, the ocean stretching out for miles before you. Now find a spot on the horizon, and keep your focus on that spot. Let's call that spot Your Future Happy Family. That spot, or YFHF, seems far away, like it would take forever to get there. But keep your focus on it. Don't let go.

That spot is your goal. Though the goal is important because it provides focus, it's not all about the goal. If you know you want a happy family, you wouldn't just get in your boat and let it drift in any direction instead of heading toward YFHF.

But how are you going to get there? You're gonna row. You're going to get in your boat and row. Every day you row. Some days you'll get three miles closer to YFHF. Some days you might go twenty feet backward. But every day you row. You wake up, put your oars in the water, and stroke, then stroke again, then stroke again. Each stroke gets you another foot, another yard, another mile closer to YFHF.

Each stroke is a decision. You're making decisions about the words you speak to yourself, your spouse, and your SKids. You're making decisions about your attitudes when your family is together, when you're at the in-laws, and when you have a date night. You're making decisions about whether you want to be right or have a great relationship. You're making decisions about embracing the baseball games and getting to know the other parents, going to the plays, concerts, and doctor's appointments.

Each stroke is an action—a pat on the back, an encouraging word, a meal together.

Goals aren't reached via instant teleportation. You don't decide, "Hey, I'm going to be an awesome SMom right NOW!" and poof! You're awesome.

No. It doesn't work that way. Goals are reached in tiny steps, with tiny decisions, one stroke of the oars at a time. You keep going. You keep striving forward. It might take months, or it might take years. But hey, time is going to pass anyway. You might as well keep moving forward. And as long as you keep your eye on YFHF and rowing in that direction, you'll get there, and all you have to do at that point is enjoy it.

Okay, maybe that's not all you have to do. You definitely have to enjoy it, but you also need to keep rowing. That's the trick about goals. Achieving the goal isn't "the thing." Everything you need to do to achieve the goal is "the thing." All of the habits you established that support YHF—the words, the attitudes, the actions—are the thing. But wowzah, look back at everything you've done and all the ways you changed and grew.

Now that you're there, you need to maintain your mindset, attitudes, and, most of all, gratitude. Appreciate this wonderful gift every day, and it will keep on giving.

Switching metaphors now; stay with me.

Imagine an old-timey playground merry-go-round. It takes a considerable effort to get it going when it's sitting still. All the kids have to stand around it and push. Once it gets going, you start hopping on. Once it really gets going, all it takes is one kid to stand there and give the bars a little push as the others go by, and it will turn and turn and turn. Or maybe you hold on tight to the bars and stick out a foot, pushing against the ground to keep you going.

Your Happy Family is like that. It takes a fair amount of effort to create it, but once you feel it, once you've "made it," then you go into maintenance mode. You enjoy the heck out of it and make sure you're pushing it here and there to keep it going.

What does this mean in the context of a family? In the beginning, you had to figure these people out. And they, you. You had to check your attitudes and make sure that only the helpful ones were expressed. You had to hold your words and filter out what would have been harmful. You had to stand your ground and ensure you were being treated well in the process. Those are the big effort strokes. Those are things you need to think about as they're happening.

But now the habits are established. The filters are automatic and mostly not even needed. Your relationships are established. You understand each other. You changed the way you operate and achieved your goal. Now, you get to enjoy it and keep giving that merry-go-round another push now and then.

OUR FAMILY NOW

After all that building, waiting, and fostering, we are a family. I'm in it. And I love it. We're so much a family that we experience normal family stuff, like the kids being annoyed at something Jason and I do, or more likely don't do. He and I don't get it right one hundred percent of the time because we're human. And the kids don't get it right one hundred percent of the time, either. But even in those times, we're a team. Minor annoyances just ping off.

Our relationships continue to evolve, as relationships do. I have watched and felt us grow closer over these six years, starting from scratch and developing into a tight-knit team. And it will be such a treat to watch where we go over the next six years.

Cassie has grown into a lovely woman, and I enjoy her humor and zest. She's spirited and a fearless advocate, and I wish I could be more like her. I love her energy and get-after-it-ness. I respect and admire her, and she respects and admires me. It's a wonderful woman-to-woman relationship where we learn from each other.

I love having this connection with Cassie. We've been able to take a more peer approach from the beginning since she was already twenty when we met. I've always viewed her as someone to learn from and enjoy as a friend. It's super fun watching her grow.

Seth serves as a source of inspiration to me. He and I are on a kind of parallel journey. I'm in a start-up company trying to change the world, and he's off in L.A. making a name for himself in the music scene. We share what it's like to do this brand new thing and forge your own way. I admire his courage and determination.

I love having this connection with Seth. It's been startling sometimes how similar our experiences have been—dejected and low on inspiration, super jacked and attacking the project, and getting major breaks all at the same time, and sometimes making our own breaks. Seth inspires me daily.

And Happy is the son I never had. But it's even better than that because we can share things that maybe you wouldn't share with your parent or with your child. Happy was young enough still when we met that I got to flex some nurturing muscles, and let me tell you, those guys were rusty.

Happy and I grew up together. He matured as a teenager and then as a young adult, and I matured as this new person in a family and as a StepMother. By just being here, Happy made me a much better person.

I love having this connection with Happy. We've figured out our relationship together, and at times, I become so overwhelmed by how I feel that I have difficulty putting words to it. Grateful is the best way I can describe how I feel about my relationship with Happy. I am very grateful to experience a taste of what it's like being a parent.

I get to be around these young adults, full of life and vigor, and watch—and help—them start their lives. Young people are fun to be around. They have so much energy. It's contagious. They inspire hope in me. And when we're all together, this family is funny. Jason is the funniest person I know, and his humor has definitely been passed down to his kids. These Charlestons keep me in stitches. They're my favorite people to be around.

We celebrate each other. All of these kids are driven to succeed, and we talk about success as a family a lot. We're all living our motto: Get after it.

In the future, when the three of them get settled where they're going to be, Jason and I talk about moving wherever they end up. I imagine Seth will be in L.A. for quite a while. Cassie and Happy are still a little bit up in the air about where they might land. It's fun to think about all of these possibilities—for them and for us.

We may just get a map, draw a triangle with each of their homes as a point, and plop down right in the center of it. And then, when it's time, I plan to be full-on Grandma. Sometimes Jason and I joke about what we'll be called. There's a pretty strong veto on Nana and MeeMaw. I'm angling for straight-up Grandma. But are the first names included? What about last names? As a kid, we always referenced our grandparents with their last name, and for a while, I declared that I would be Grandma Suess.

My Grandma Suess was wonderful. I spent a lot of time with her, cutting quilt squares (worst job) and eating homemade bread (best job). She was warm and soft and sang silly little songs. She played the piano (pronouncing it like py-ANN-ah), and I would sing along.

But then, somebody said it. It must have been a conversation about possible grandparent names for Jason and me, and someone called me Grandma Suess. It was strange. Grandma Suess is such a specific and wonderful persona that I can't live up to it. I do fantasize about always having homemade cookies for the kids, and then I remember how much sugar kids have and how I was NOT going to contribute to that, and MY grandkids are getting whole wheat pancakes and fruit for snacks, gosh darn it. I might be setting myself up to be the least favorite grandma.

I do have a GrandDog, and he knows me as Grandma T. That's not so bad. I think any form of Grandma would be delightful. I'm sure it won't even matter once those little ones arrive, which is hopefully a few years away. I'd love some time with us all as adults before the babies come.

Jason is expressing how he misses the time when the kids needed him more. He's going to be a wonderful grandpa. I'm excited to watch that unfold. And I'm very much looking forward to being a regular old grandma to my StepKids' kids.

REFLECTION QUESTIONS

- What kind of energy does our home have? If it isn't the vibe we want, what changes can we make to improve it?
- If I'm new to this home and family, do I respect the culture that existed before me? If not, in what ways am I trying to change it prematurely?
- Does our family have a motto? If not, brainstorm some family mottos and see if one works for our family.
- When I envision my YFHF, what do I want it to look and feel like?
- What five small decisions can I make to row myself toward my goal?

CHRISTMAS 2022

"How was your Christmas?"

"10/10. It was wonderful. Best Christmas ever."

Christmas is a major project that requires at least one spreadsheet and two other hand-written supplemental lists. Who gets in when? Gifts and budgets. Freshening up the guest rooms. Where we need to be and when. Food, food, and more food.

What day is Seth flying in?

What days are you working?

What are we feeding everybody?

What should I take to Mom's?

When are we going to your brother's?

We have to run the Roomba.

I like it, honestly. It's a lot of moving pieces to put together, and I enjoy the process of gathering those pieces, tracking them, making a plan, and then executing it. Christmas 2022 was so beautifully planned and executed that the whole experience was a pleasure.

It starts with scheduling, which typically happens in October. We get all the families sorted out and figure out when everyone is meeting and how we can coordinate that with the kids' other gatherings. Then Jason and Seth secure Seth's travel plans, so he's here for as much of the doings as possible.

Once December hits, it's go time. Jason and I split up the chores this year, which was a godsend. He handled freshening the two guest rooms while I managed the food planning and gift lists. I had this down to what time of day things should happen. It was beautiful. The planning was so thorough that I didn't even need the schedule by the time we were in the middle of execution. Everything was prepped, labeled, and ready. Christmas 2022 was a testament to the power of planning.

Seth arrived. Then Cassie, her beau Bob, and little dog Franklin arrived. We had our C-Unit Christmas (that's what I call ourselves, shortened from the Charleston Unit) the night before Christmas Eve. I don't love that we have to fit that in around everything else—I think it should be the priority, and everything else fits around it—but that's where we are at this stage of life.

Presents or dinner first? We got different answers to this question, so Jason declared a vote. The declaration of a vote is always amusing because the kids tease Jason that no matter how they vote, it will be what Jason says anyway. But the vote went on. Three hands for presents first. Three hands for dinner first. Look at that: Jason is the tie vote. Presents first it is!

We did the ol' one person opens at a time, which was delightful because all the gifts were great, and it was a pleasure to watch everyone unwrap them. I was proud of the gifts we presented this year. Watching their faces as they opened them filled my heart. Plus, the kids and Jason both did an awesome job buying for me. Michael Kors sunglasses? Beats headphones? Um, excuse me. I'll be in my trailer.

In the glow of this gift experience, the dinner preparations began. I have come to greatly enjoy making meals for this crew when we're all together, and I was especially excited about this one. Brunch was the menu—my pick since I'm confident with breakfast foods and insecure about beef, ham, and whole birds.

Egg bake, breakfast sliders, bacon, hash browns, chocolate chip pancakes, toast, fruit, mimosas. I mean, come on. That's an awesome lineup right there.

I was in bliss engaging with food, creating delicious dishes for my favorite people, all while listening to them talk, laugh, tease, and try to set up a table and chairs in a room that wasn't quite big enough.

Jason sprang into action with the pancakes and put Seth on hash brown duty while Bob volunteered to be the toastmaster (my father-in-law's toast is the best in the world, so anyone attempting to make toast for the family has big shoes to fill).

The kitchen and living room were full, as were our hearts.

It was time to eat! We sat at a beautifully set table, our plates piled with delicious-looking food, our mouths ready to devour the last ninety minutes of effort. Happy took a bite.

"Before we eat," Jason said, clearly starting a speech. Happy dropped his fork with a cat-eating-the-canary look on his face. "I'd like to say a few words."

Jason likes to make short speeches to the family when we're together—a Christmas toast or a thoughtful expression at the July Fourth celebration. His love language is words, and he makes sure we all know how much we mean to him as often as he can. We could tell this speech would be a bit longer than his usual two or three sentences, which always included my favorite saying of his: "You have my full love and support at all times."

In the festive blue light of the Christmas tree, the wafting scents of candles, and the piles of delicious food and drink before us, Jason expressed his love and gratitude for his family, starting with a phrase we've heard before and another favorite of mine: "You should never have to wonder or worry whether your father loves you or not."

There were these tiny little pauses as he talked, the classic indicator of emotion. He was touched, and so were we all, by his words.

He asked us then to all offer a similar expression. What was meaningful to us at that moment? One by one, each person declared their love and thankfulness for this family, how we show up for each other, and how we support each other. Each person has their own path, and this team walks with them, cheering them on.

The speeches were absolutely lovely, each one pulling at our heartstrings, every word building on the deep emotions in the room, pulling us all closer together.

I was last to speak, so I had plenty of time to think about what I would say. I silently practiced the first sentence over and over while listening to the words of my family. I couldn't get beyond that first sentence in my mind since my attention was more focused outward. And, as it turned out, I couldn't get beyond that first sentence out loud either.

"If someone had told me, seven years ago, that seven years from now, I would be excitedly planning a Christmas weekend, and all my StepKids would be coming ..." I felt the emotion coming to the surface. *Damn it! I really wanted to get through this speech.* I turned my head toward Jason. "... and that I would be married to ..." Eye contact. Wrong move. I lost it. I could no longer speak. But I didn't care. I had to finish.

I didn't finish exactly because I had no words prepared after the seven years part. So I paused for a moment, took a breath, looked at everyone, and shared my most dear thought through a cracked voice, scrunched face, and words broken by emotion.

"This family is the greatest joy of my life."

Whew! I said it!

There was not a dry eye in the house at that point. We raised our glasses to commemorate the moment, and the air broke with announcements about how much everyone was crying. We laughed together as each person retold watching me look at Jason and becoming overwhelmed with emotion themselves. They knew it was coming, they said.

That moment, the dinner, the speeches, the emotion, the laughter, and the love shared among us all truly brought us closer together. We grew our bond that evening in a way that punctuated our whole experience to that point. We knew, in that moment, that we had made it.

Our story together will never end. Eventually, we'll see marriages, babies, cross-country moves, job changes, and the unfortunate passing of those we love. How do I close a book about the joy of Stepping when the Stepping will continue, and more stories will be written?

Here. The book ends here at Christmas 2022. It was the culmination of six years of building ourselves together. Of finding out how we'll live together, how we'll work together, how we'll be together as a family. We're set now. The opening story has concluded. On to the next chapter.

TO THE KIDS WITH DIFFICULT STEPPARENTS

This season of life is temporary. You won't be living with your StepParents forever. There will be a time when you are in complete control of your own life.

Other people won't intervene on your behalf because that's not what others do. You may not understand this until later in life, but people tend not to get involved in other families' situations. It's not that they don't love you and want you to be well—they absolutely do. People tend to act in their own self-interest, and getting involved in someone else's family can go against that.

You are still loved in the world. You are still valued in the world. You are still needed in the world.

None of it is about you. Everything other people say and do comes from their own thoughts, filters, and interpretations. If someone is mean to you, it's not because you deserve it. It's because something is happening in themselves and spilling out onto you. It's not about you at all. You happen to be the person there.

People who are mean to others do so because they hurt inside. Whole, complete, happy people aren't arbitrarily assholes. If you can, separate yourself from their behavior and see if you can find compassion for their pain. I know that's a big ask, especially when that person's inner pain is getting all over you.

It's your job to stay a whole person. Once you are no longer living with your difficult Step, it's up to you to heal and make your own path. Once you're not living with your Step, all your decisions are yours. That means taking responsibility for your life, thoughts, and feelings.

Do the best you can to stay clear in your own mind. Journal, meditate, talk to people you trust, and advocate for yourself when you need to.

This is temporary, and it's not about you.

From *The Power of Moments: Why Certain Experiences Have Extraordinary Impact* by Chip Heath and Dan Heath:

> "We are accustomed to thinking about relationships in terms of time: The longer the relationship endures, the closer it must grow. But relationships don't proceed in steady, predictable increments. There's no guarantee that they will deepen with time. When you and your uncle make the same small talk every Thanksgiving, it's not a surprise that ten years later, you don't feel any closer. Conversely, have you ever met someone and felt instantly that you like and trusted them?
>
> What we'll see is that if we can create the right kind of moment, relationships can change in an instant."

QUOTES

"My husband stepped into that StepFather role when my kids were five and ten. And having something like this as a guide in some ways would have been helpful. Just that parenting agreement, I went, Oh! We never really talked about it. It evolved, especially with one being so young—they're great buddies and really connected, but my other one being closer to teenage years, took more work and more effort.

Theresa

About the Author

Tricia Suess Charleston is an entrepreneur with a deep-rooted understanding of step relationships, having been part of them since she was 8 years old. Her personal experiences have shaped her expertise in step parenting, making her a compassionate and insightful voice on the subject. Tricia lives in southern Wisconsin with her husband, where she enjoys reading, traveling, laughing with friends and cherishing moments with her family—mostly because they provide her with endless material for her stories. Her book, "Step'ping Up," reflects her commitment to helping others navigate the StepParent role with grace, wisdom, and a good sense of humor.

Appendix

RECOMMENDED BOOKS:

These three books will deliver the same concepts, told in slightly different ways:

Clear, James. *Atomic Habits: An Easy & Proven Way to Build Good Habits & Break Bad Ones.* New York: Avery, 2018. *Atomic Habits* digs into how to form a new habit or stop an old one.

Hardy, Darren. *The Compound Effect.* New York: Hachette Go, 2010.

Olson, Jeff. *The Slight Edge: Turning Simple Disciplines into Massive Success.* Texas: Success Books, 2011.

Other great books that have helped me on my path:

Avery, Christopher. *The Responsibility Process: Unlocking Your Natural Ability to Live and Lead with Power.* Texas: Partnerwerks, 2016.

Heath, Chip, and Dan Heath. *The Power of Moments: Why Certain Experiences Have Extraordinary Impact.* New York: Simon & Schuster, 2017.

Ruiz, Don Miguel. *The Four Agreements: A Practical Guide to Personal Freedom.* California: Amber-Allen Publishing, 1997. *The Four Agreements* helps us learn how not to take anything personally.

Sincero, Jen. *You Are a Badass: How to Stop Doubting Your Greatness and Start Living an Awesome Life.* New York: Running Press Adult, 2013.

Yeah, man, let's step.

Printed in the United States
by Baker & Taylor Publisher Services